ork Times.

PROBABLY 1,250 DEAD;
AST; SINKS IN 15 MINUTES;
N AND VANDERBILT MISSING;
T A GRAVE CRISIS IS AT HAND

SOME DEAD TAKEN ASHORE

Several Hundred Story
ors at Queenstown
and Kinsale.

NOTICE

Unraveling
FREEDOM

Unraveling FREEDOM

 ### The Battle for Democracy on the Home Front During World War I

ANN BAUSUM

NATIONAL GEOGRAPHIC

WASHINGTON, D.C.

For Kedron

PUBLISHED BY THE NATIONAL GEOGRAPHIC SOCIETY

John M. Fahey, Jr., *President and Chief Executive Officer*

Gilbert M. Grosvenor, *Chairman of the Board*

Tim T. Kelly, *President, Global Media Group*

John Q. Griffin, *Executive Vice President; President, Publishing*

Nina D. Hoffman, *Executive Vice President; President, Book Publishing Group*

Melina Gerosa Bellows, *Executive Vice President, Children's Publishing*

PREPARED BY THE BOOK DIVISION

Nancy Laties Feresten, *Vice President, Editor in Chief, Children's Books*

Jonathan Halling, *Design Director, Children's Publishing*

Jennifer Emmett, *Executive Editor, Reference and Solo, Children's Books*

Carl Mehler, *Director of Maps*

R. Gary Colbert, *Production Director*

Jennifer A. Thornton, *Managing Editor*

STAFF FOR THIS BOOK

Jennifer Emmett, *Editor*

Jim Hiscott, *Art Director*

Lori Epstein, *Illustrations Editor*

Marty Ittner, *Designer*

Kate Olesin, *Editorial Assistant*

Grace Hill, *Associate Managing Editor*

Lewis R. Bassford, *Production Manager*

Susan Borke, *Legal and Business Affairs*

MANUFACTURING AND QUALITY MANAGEMENT

Christopher A. Liedel, *Chief Financial Officer*

Phillip L. Schlosser, *Vice President*

Chris Brown, *Technical Director*

Nicole Elliott, *Manager*

Rachel Faulise, *Manager*

A NOTE ON THE DESIGN

The design inspiration for *Unraveling Freedom* is drawn from the propaganda posters of World War I. You'll see examples of these bold, graphic pieces on pages 29 and 40. The title text for the book is set in Trade Gothic and Marmalade, and the body text is set in Minion Pro. The palette for the book echoes the colors of the American flag—red, white, and blue. To add new life to old photographs and to draw the eye to the central subject matter of an image, some of the pictures in the book (see, for example, page 39) are silhouetted with a special digital technique that pulls the subject of the photograph forward in the frame, while the background is tinted with a color. The colored diagonal design elements, and the frequent angling of the images contribute to a sense of disruption, of things being off balance. This feeling echoes the turbulent sentiment of the times, brought on by the first global war and the erosion of liberties on the home front.

Echoes of history. The September 11, 2001 terrorist attacks on the United States (closing endpapers, headline news) prompted the nation's entry into wars in Iraq and Afghanistan; almost a century earlier, the sinking of the *Lusitania* helped propel the United States toward combat during World War I. The *New York Times* coverage of the 1915 maritime disaster (opening endpapers) reproduced a German warning of possible attacks (lower right, headlined "NOTICE!").

The graphic foreword by Ted Rall, President of the Association of American Editorial Cartoonists, evokes the era of political cartooning that flourished during World War I.

Library of Congress Cataloging-in-Publication Data

Bausum, Ann.

 Unraveling freedom : the battle for democracy on the home front during World War I / by Ann Bausum.

   p. cm.

 Includes bibliographical references and index.

 ISBN 978-1-4263-0702-7 (hardcover : alk. paper) -- ISBN 978-1-4263-0703-4 (library binding : alk. paper)

 1. United States--Politics and government--1913-1921--Juvenile literature. 2. World War, 1914-1918--Social aspects--United States--Juvenile literature. 3. German Americans--Social conditions--20th century--Juvenile literature. I. Title.

 E780.B38 2010

 940.3'73--dc22

                                              2010010631

Printed in China

10/RRDS/1

CONTENTS

FOREWORD

BY TED RALL

THE WORLD WILL LITTLE NOTE, NOR LONG REMEMBER WHAT WE SAY HERE, BUT IT CAN NEVER FORGET WHAT THEY DID HERE.

WAR BRINGS OUT THE BEST IN A COUNTRY.

GETTYSBURG, PA, CIVIL WAR, 1863

IT ALSO BRINGS OUT THE WORST.

SAIGON, VIETNAM, 1968

WAR MAKES COUNTRIES CRAZY.

INSTRUCTIONS TO ALL PERSONS OF JAPANESE ANCESTRY

NOTICE

SAN FRANCISCO, CA, 1942

AFTER A WAR IS OVER, PEOPLE CAN HARDLY BELIEVE THEY EVER DID SUCH THINGS.

6

7

Ted Rall is President of the Association of American Editorial Cartoonists. Visit him online at: http://www.rall.com/

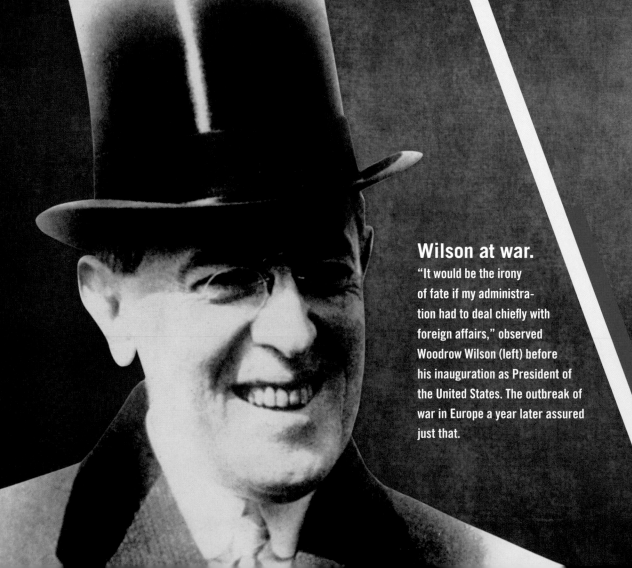

"*We shall* **fight** *for the things which we have always carried nearest to our* hearts [until we] *make the world itself at last* free."

WOODROW WILSON, CONCLUDING REMARKS FROM HIS WAR MESSAGE TO CONGRESS, APRIL 2, 1917

Wilson at war.
"It would be the irony of fate if my administration had to deal chiefly with foreign affairs," observed Woodrow Wilson (left) before his inauguration as President of the United States. The outbreak of war in Europe a year later assured just that.

INTRODUCTION

IN THE SPRING OF 1917, as the United States prepared to declare war on

Germany and enter the fight that would become known as World War I, perhaps

as many as a quarter of all Americans had either been born in Germany or

had descended from Germans. My grandfather was one of them. But Frederic

William Bausum and his family could be considered some of the lucky German-

Americans on the eve of war. They spoke English and had no divided loyalty to

an old-world country. They had grown up in the United States, married across

ethnic lines, homesteaded on the Western plains, and embraced the customs

and beliefs of the country. They had, in short, become Americanized.

English Bulldog

German Dachshund

American Bull Terrier

I'm Neutral, BUT-Not Afraid of any of them.

Thousands of other German-Americans were less fortunate. Almost overnight, the language they spoke by birth, the relatives they retained ties to from their past, the books they read, the schools they attended, even the food and drink they found most familiar and enjoyable, all became associated with the enemy: Germany.

Immigrants and descendants from other places bore ties to competing nations, too, from Great Britain to France to Italy to Russia. U.S. residents who shared backgrounds and beliefs with these countries found themselves taking sides in the conflict at home even as President Woodrow Wilson tried to steer the United States away from joining the conflict abroad. Finally, on April 2, 1917, the President addressed Congress and made a dramatic appeal for the nation to enter the fight. In words that continue to be quoted for their eloquence and passion, Wilson asserted that "the world must be made safe for democracy."

Yet, in one of the greatest ironies of 20th century U.S. history, the President so committed to securing democracy and freedom abroad failed to prevent the unraveling of freedom in his own country. Even as millions of Americans put on military uniforms and as the nation expended billions of dollars to fund the fight, freedom came under siege in the United States.

French Bulldog

Russian Wolf-Hound

WALLACE ROBINSON—191

Dogs in the fight. Even though the United States remained neutral after fighting broke out in Europe in 1914, Americans followed the conflict between the continent's leading nations with concern. Dogs became symbols for competing countries, with dachshunds representing Germany. The American bull terrier (third from left) personified a confident and fearless stand by the United States.

New laws tested the rights of individuals to question and criticize the government. Leaders who spoke from the edges of the political spectrum found themselves ridiculed, harassed, even jailed. A government-sponsored propaganda effort built public support for the war by fanning anti-immigrant feelings within the nation. At a time when Americans fought abroad in the name of freedom and democracy, Americans at home burned German-language books, put German-language newspapers out of business, condemned German foods and drinks, and spied on fellow citizens, especially those with ancestral ties to Germany.

Some of these wrongs took decades to right. Others forever altered the nature of American life—from the nation's commitment to teaching foreign languages to its tolerance of differences in people from foreign lands. What happens when a segment of the population can be charged with disloyalty simply because of its heritage? Why may democracy go off track when national security seems at risk? How can a nation of immigrants, whose strength comes in part from its diversity, survive the internal conflicts that follow when wars develop with old homelands?

One needs only to look back at history to find questions—and answers—that echo from the past into events of modern times.

"The ship was sinking with unbelievable rapidity. There was a terrible panic *on her deck. It was the most terrible sight I have ever seen. . . . The scene was too* horrible *to watch."*

CAPTAIN WALTHER SCHWIEGER, OF *U-BOAT 20*, AFTER FIRING A TORPEDO AT THE *LUSITANIA*

SUNK

T TOOK ONLY 18 MINUTES for the great ship to sink. Even the *Titanic* had lingered on the ocean surface for more than two hours before sliding to the bottom of the Atlantic in 1912. But, on a sunny spring afternoon just three years later, the *Lusitania* began to list toward her starboard side almost immediately after being struck by a single submarine-fired torpedo. Minutes later she was gone.

The British ship had been within sight of the Irish coast when U-boat Captain Walther Schwieger commanded his German crew to launch a torpedo at the ocean liner as it steamed past, perhaps 2,300 feet away. It was 2:10 in the afternoon on May 7, 1915. Germany, England,

Going down!
As the *Lusitania* sank, the surrounding water became filled with "waving hands and arms belonging to struggling men and frantic women and children," according to one survivor. The sea "was black with people," observed another.

and other European powers had been at war for nine months. Most of the *Lusitania's* 1,257 passengers, having eaten their last lunch of the journey, were anticipating their arrival in England the next morning when the 20-foot-long torpedo struck their ship broadside, punching a large hole in the giant vessel's midsection.

★ CAPTAIN SCHWIEGER, HIS CREW OF 34 MEN, and their adopted litter of dachshund puppies had been at sea a week when the *Lusitania* appeared in the sights of the submarine's periscope. By then the crew had already attacked several smaller ships, sinking three and expending four of the sub's seven torpedoes. Two of the remaining three weapons were to be held in emergency reserve for the return trip to Germany, leaving one torpedo available for an attack.

The *Lusitania* proved to be an easy target. Despite assurances that she would be greeted in home waters by an armed escort, no such protection materialized as she approached her destination of Liverpool, England, either because none had been requested or because none could be spared by the British Navy. At full speed the *Lusitania* could easily have outrun any German submarine, but wartime economies had closed one of her four boiler rooms, and the ship's captain had further reduced her speed for navigation purposes.

Captain William Turner had commanded the *Lusitania* for only a few months of the ship's eight-year history, but he had sailed for more than three decades with the vessel's Cunard Line owner. The 30,000-ton

15

Battles on the seas. The *Lusitania* (top, anchored at New York City in 1907) was one of the world's fastest ships and symbolized Great Britain's sea savvy. When World War I broke out, Great Britain had the largest fleet of military submarines (75 boats). Germany had only 28 U-boats, short for *Unterseeboot* or underwater boat, but her subs were of more modern design (middle, *U-boat 14*). Early in the war Walther Schwieger (right), captain of *U-boat 20*, attacked and sank the *Lusitania*.

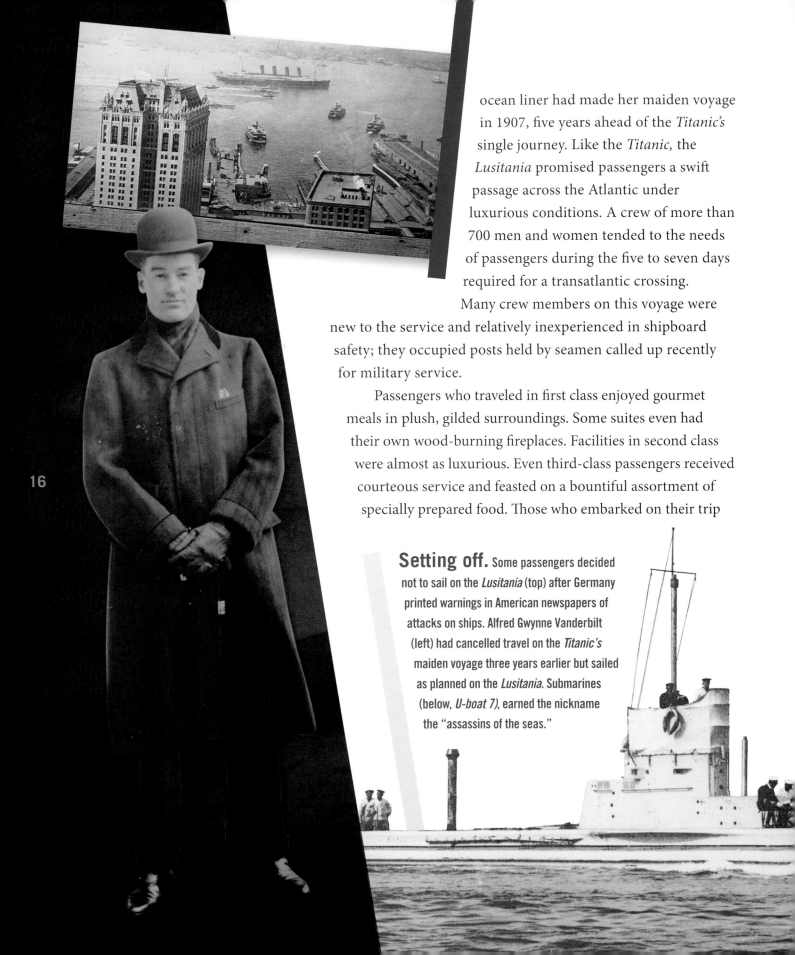

ocean liner had made her maiden voyage in 1907, five years ahead of the *Titanic's* single journey. Like the *Titanic,* the *Lusitania* promised passengers a swift passage across the Atlantic under luxurious conditions. A crew of more than 700 men and women tended to the needs of passengers during the five to seven days required for a transatlantic crossing.

Many crew members on this voyage were new to the service and relatively inexperienced in shipboard safety; they occupied posts held by seamen called up recently for military service.

Passengers who traveled in first class enjoyed gourmet meals in plush, gilded surroundings. Some suites even had their own wood-burning fireplaces. Facilities in second class were almost as luxurious. Even third-class passengers received courteous service and feasted on a bountiful assortment of specially prepared food. Those who embarked on their trip

Setting off. Some passengers decided not to sail on the *Lusitania* (top) after Germany printed warnings in American newspapers of attacks on ships. Alfred Gwynne Vanderbilt (left) had cancelled travel on the *Titanic's* maiden voyage three years earlier but sailed as planned on the *Lusitania.* Submarines (below, *U-boat 7),* earned the nickname the "assassins of the seas."

from the harbor in New York City on May 1, 1915, included the usual complement of celebrities and millionaires. Most notable, perhaps, was Alfred Gwynne Vanderbilt, descendant of the railroad magnate; he was one of about 200 other Americans bound for England on the *Lusitania*. Most of the rest of the passengers were British or Canadian. Everyone knew that this transatlantic crossing carried added risks because of the new European war.

In August 1914, soon after Allied forces from such nations as England and France pushed back against Germany's invasion of Belgium, the Germans began attacking enemy ships with submarines. Submarine warfare was a new idea then, and there was not yet a code of conduct for using this new technology. Which ships could be attacked? Warships, clearly yes. But what about merchant ships carrying cargo and supplies to enemy countries? Or boats that carried passengers and cargo? Should vessels be forewarned of attack so that they could be evacuated? Or could subs attack without warning? Answers remained unclear, and unease developed in February 1915 after Germany announced that it would begin using submarines to attack other ships, whatever their nationality, if they approached British ports. Since then the Germans had sunk 66 commercial ships; 23 had been attacked just since the *Lusitania's* departure from New York.

Thus, the first glimpses by passengers of the Irish coast on the morning of May 7 signified both the nearness of their destination and their arrival in dangerous waters. Many people were on one of the *Lusitania's* open-air decks as Captain Schwieger prepared to fire at the passing target. A number of survivors could recall their horror upon glimpsing the silhouette of *U-boat 20's* periscope above the calm, sunny ocean. They and others stood mesmerized as they realized that the trail of bubbles advancing toward them marked the unstoppable track of a torpedo set to reach its target in less than a minute's time. Most on board remained oblivious to the approaching danger until they heard and felt the impact of the torpedo.

Captain Schwieger had aimed his torpedo with dead-on accuracy. Had he fired five seconds sooner or 20 seconds later, the weapon would have skimmed past the liner entirely. As it was, the missile hit the ship broadside, inflicting the maximum possible damage and triggering a sequence of catastrophic injuries to the liner. Some substance—probably coal dust—exploded almost immediately after the torpedo struck, widening the hole in the boat's side. Thousands of gallons of water began rushing into the *Lusitania*, causing her to list toward the wound on her starboard side. Additional seawater poured in through open portholes and hatches as they fell below the water line, further dragging the ship off balance. Immediately the captain and crew found themselves without enough power or control to stop the vessel's forward momentum or steer it toward shore.

Within minutes, the ship's electrical power system failed, plunging passengers and crew still below decks into darkness. Passengers traveling to the upper decks inside electrically powered elevators found themselves permanently trapped. Crew members working in the deepest bowels of the boat—in areas only reachable by electric elevators—became cut off from all reasonable means of escape.

Even those standing on exterior decks faced uncertain exits from the ship. The *Titanic* tragedy assured that vessels now had ample lifeboats and life jackets, but most life jackets were stowed in passenger cabins, causing people to rush back and forth down crowded and (within minutes) darkened passageways to find them. As the ship listed to one side, baby carriages, some still occupied by infants, careened across the boat's decks. Furniture, potted plants, and dishes spilled or broke, leaving decks, cabins, and passageways littered with debris. Halls and stairs became obstacle courses as the increasing slant of the ship upended their usual orientations.

★ THE LACK OF A PUBLIC ADDRESS SYSTEM

complicated efforts to establish an orderly evacuation of the liner. So did the increasing list of the *Lusitania* toward its wounded starboard side. Lifeboats hanging on this side of the ship swung away from the deck, almost out of reach. As incoming seawater caused the liner's bow to sink, the bows of the hanging lifeboats dipped, too, leaving them cockeyed and harder to lower. Many of the seamen trained at launching lifeboats remained trapped below decks. Those who attempted it repeatedly failed to coordinate the complicated effort, dumping the lifeboats' human cargo—principally women and children—into the ocean.

Meanwhile the listing of the ship caused lifeboats on the *Lusitania*'s port side to bump against the vessel's exterior hull as they were lowered, spilling evacuees into the sea. Often then the empty boats crashed down on victims below. In the end, many passengers

"*It was freely stated and generally believed that a special effort was to be made to* sink [the Lusitania] *so as to inspire the* world with terror."

MARGARET MACKWORTH, PASSENGER ON THE *LUSITANIA'S* FINAL VOYAGE

SOS! "Come at once," signaled the *Lusitania's* wireless operator after the ship was attacked by a German U-boat (below, a torpedo). No photographs were made of the sinking ship, so artists dramatized the scene (left). The *New York Herald* called the sinking "premeditated slaughter," but Germans defended the attack, charging that the ship secretly carried war supplies, a claim that the Allies denied.

On dry land. Survivors (above) struggled to comprehend the trauma they had experienced during the sinking of the *Lusitania*. Some reflexively refused to give up their life jackets (opposite page). Sorting the living from the dead could be challenging. "Good gracious, are you alive?" asked a startled rescuer after a bellboy from the ship sat up amongst a pile of corpses.

and crew members simply jumped into the water. Others were swept overboard. Countless more remained trapped on board when the ship sank out of sight at 2:28 p.m.

A life jacket did not necessarily assure safety in the water. Many people, in panic or ignorance, had put the devices on upside down or backward. Thus the jacket promptly flipped its wearer head first or face down in the water. Floating wreckage offered sanctuary for some but created life-and-death battles among others. People clung to anything that floated, including dead bodies. Calls for help, screams, and the cries of children filled the air around an ever-widening circle of debris floating in blood-red waters. The chill of the spring Atlantic—probably about 52 degrees— shortened the chances of survival for children and the elderly. Even the hardiest faced death by hypothermia within hours of immersion, if not sooner.

Scenes of wrenching separation and miraculous reunions punctuated the chaotic minutes of the ship's sinking and the hours of waiting and rescue that followed. Gerda Nielson and John Welsh, who had fallen in love during their journey, were pulled from the water by occupants of a passing lifeboat. Norah Bretherton, a mother traveling alone in second class with two young children, was with neither one of them when the torpedo struck. She found, then lost track of, her 15-month-old daughter before escaping with her son in a lifeboat.

Captain Schwieger's U-boat was long gone by the time the first rescue ship arrived at the field of floating debris about three and a half hours after the *Lusitania* had sunk. It took until 8 p.m. for an initial boatload of survivors to travel some 12 miles from the wreckage to the Irish seaport of Queenstown, the impromptu home base for rescue efforts. David Thomas, a former member of the British Parliament, was standing on the docks at 11 p.m., scanning the faces of survivors, when his grown daughter Margaret Mackworth struggled ashore. The pair had become separated following the attack. Captain Turner, who had jumped from his ship as she sank and been pulled from the wreckage hours later, arrived on the same boat. More vessels followed.

★ BIZARRE STORIES OF SURVIVAL

abounded, including the case of Margaret Gwyer who, upon entering the water, found herself sucked into one of the ship's four smokestack funnels as the *Lusitania* sank, only to be forcibly expelled from it moments later by a blast of steam from an exploding boiler. She survived, albeit minus most of her clothes and coated in soot and grease. Ian McDermott, shoveling coal in boiler room number two at the time of the attack, found himself washed to safety by seawater that swept through the ship and exited through the room's ventilation shaft. Parry Jones, a member of a singing group returning from a North American tour, survived an eight-hour stay in the water.

George Hook and his adolescent son and daughter had jumped from the *Lusitania's* decks, but had become separated. Father and daughter feared the boy dead even as the son assumed he'd lost them; they were reunited in a Queenstown hospital. The Morton brothers, *Lusitania* deckhands, presumed each other lost until they coincidentally inspected opposite ends of the same dead body in a makeshift mortuary. Avis Dolphin, a 12-year-old Canadian on her way to school in England, credited her survival to a friendly Scottish professor who had personally tied on her life jacket, an act that became crucial after her lifeboat capsized and dumped her into the water. When last seen by Professor Ian Holbourn, Avis was being sucked underwater in the *Lusitania's* wake. She surfaced soon after, and the friends met again in Queenstown.

Remembering the dead.

Nearly 150 bodies recovered from the *Lusitania* could not be identified. They were buried in one of three mass graves (above) on the outskirts of Queenstown. Coffins were in short supply locally; more had to be shipped in from other cities. The bodies of Americans were returned to the United States unless relatives requested that they be buried in Ireland. Artists drew countless cartoons about the attack on the *Lusitania*. Many emphasized the innocence of the youngest victims and the ship's poor defenses, no better than toy cannons (right).

The mounting collection of bodies—stacked at first like cordwood and then laid out in makeshift morgues—made the day's losses very real and very horrifying. Corpses with missing limbs and disfigured faces revealed the brutality of the final moments of life and the natural ravages of even a few hours spent in the ocean. Seagulls pecked out eyes. Scavenging fish ate away limbs. Torsos turned up without heads. Intact bodies became bloated with seawater. As gruesome as the task was of identifying the dead—and some bodies could not be identified at all—the presence of a corpse brought closure to surviving family members. The absence of a body left friends and loved ones on edge, hoping for a miraculous recovery of someone at an isolated point on the Irish coast or among those unidentified survivors housed at area hotels and hospitals.

Among the missing were Alfred Vanderbilt, observed by many in the act of helping others during the *Lusitania's* final chaotic minutes above the surface. Charlotte Pye attested that Vanderbilt had taken off his own life jacket and placed it on her before helping her enter a lifeboat with her infant daughter. The millionaire's body was never recovered. Neither were the bodies of most of the dead. Even though corpses washed ashore in the weeks after the sinking, some 900 people remained missing and were never seen again. Still-fresh memories from the accidental sinking of the *Titanic* three years earlier may have made reports of the *Lusitania's* destruction that much more grim and vivid. About two-thirds of the 1,962 individuals who sailed on the *Lusitania's* final voyage perished, including 785 passengers and 413 crew members. Just 35 out of 129 children survived; nearly all infants perished. A total of 128 Americans lost their lives.

News of the catastrophe spread rapidly by way of telegraphed messages and phone calls. Soon banner headlines on both continents began to convey the horrors experienced by survivors, the extensive loss of life, and the almost immediate destruction of what had been considered, like the *Titanic,* to be an unsinkable ship. It did not take long for the tragedy to be transformed into a battle cry that would help inflame and expand the European conflict into the First World War. That cry echoed from shore to shore. It was passed along through newspapers, plastered onto military recruitment posters, and evoked with passion from the halls of the British Parliament to the chambers of the United States Capitol. And it rang from the voices of Allied soldiers as they charged across European battlefields. The voices rose and swelled into an enduring chorus: "Remember the *Lusitania!*"

War work. Few experiences in Woodrow Wilson's life prepared him to be a wartime Commander in Chief while President of the United States. He had rarely traveled, never served in the armed forces, and barely studied military history.

"We must throw the influence of this nation *in behalf of a plan.... This is the part I think you are destined to play in this* world tragedy, *and it is the noblest part that has ever come to a son of man."*

EDWARD M. HOUSE, ADVISING WOODROW WILSON TO TAKE AMERICA TO WAR, 1915

A CALL TO ARMS

BEFORE MAY 7, 1915, few people really believed that German subs could catch and attack the mighty *Lusitania,* or that German officers would dare to fire at the passenger ship without warning, or that the vessel could be destroyed so completely and rapidly. Such concepts were unthinkable, beyond imagination, in much the same way that few people anticipated the calculated and catastrophic terrorist attacks of September 11, 2001, on New York City's World Trade Center and other U.S. sites. The sinking of the *Lusitania* was the 9-11 of its time, and, like 9-11, it served as a backdrop as the United States moved toward war. Perhaps the most remarkable difference in the case of the *Lusitania* is that so much time passed between calamity and combat.

Wilson speaks out.

Woodrow Wilson was the first U.S. President since John Adams to formally address Congress. He made repeated speeches there during his Presidency, including his 1917 appeal for war (near right). Wilson wrote his own speeches, often typing them himself on his portable typewriter. He proposed to his future second wife, Edith Bolling Galt (far right), just days before the *Lusitania's* sinking. His first wife had died the same month that war broke out in Europe.

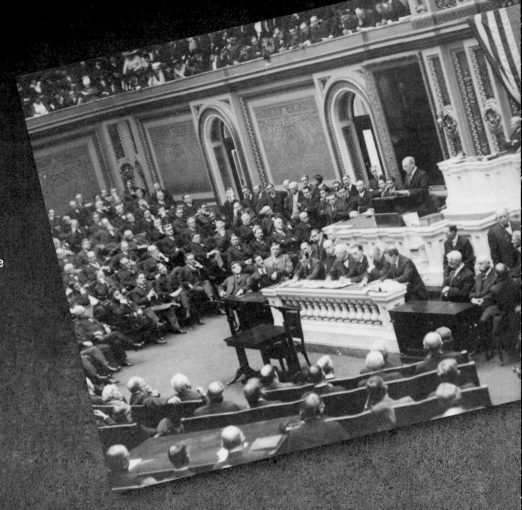

26

"*The day* has come *when America is privileged to spend her blood and her might for the* principles *that gave her birth and happiness....* God helping her, she can do no other."

Finally, on the evening of April 2, 1917, legislators filled the chairs of the House of Representatives and guests packed the seats of its balcony to hear Woodrow Wilson call the nation to take up arms. The President's call came nearly two years after the loss of the *Lusitania* because Germany had begun to violate safe passage agreements that had followed the 1915 sinking. Among those attending was the Democratic President's new wife, Edith, whom he had married just 16 months earlier. Others present included two senators who did not support the move toward war, Wisconsin Senator Robert La Follette and James Vardaman from Mississippi; unlike their colleagues, neither man wore American flag pins on their jacket lapels. Massachusetts Senator Henry Cabot Lodge, a staunch advocate for war, did. Regardless of political opinion, expectations ran high that the President—who prided himself on his public speaking ability—would deliver a stirring address. He did not disappoint.

"The present submarine warfare against commerce is a warfare against mankind," Wilson asserted. "I advise that the Congress declare the recent course of the Imperial German Government to be in fact nothing less than war against the Government and the people of the United States."

Wilson presented the coming conflict in lofty and noble terms. "We are glad . . . to fight thus for the ultimate peace of the world and for the liberation of its peoples," he proclaimed. The United States should fight "for the rights of nations great and small and the privilege of men everywhere to choose their way of life and of obedience. The world must be made safe for democracy. . . . We shall be satisfied when [the rights of mankind] have been made as secure as the faith and the freedom of nations can make them."

The audience rose in a standing ovation as Wilson concluded his speech. Robert Lansing, Wilson's second Secretary of State, described the President's performance. "From the moment that he entered the auditorium up to the time that he passed out into the corridors of the Capitol he was master of the situation," he observed. "His control of language and of his audience was a marvelous exhibition of his genius as an orator."

Even former President Theodore Roosevelt, a fierce political opponent of Wilson's, visited the White House within days of the speech and told Wilson that his words might "rank . . . with the great state papers of Washington and Lincoln." A columnist for the *New York Times* commented that "the sole defect of this great and noble message is its date." The writer, like Roosevelt, regretted that Wilson's call for war had not "swiftly followed the crime of the *Lusitania*."

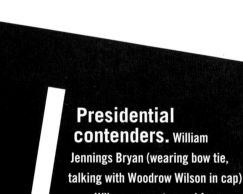

Presidential contenders. William Jennings Bryan (wearing bow tie, talking with Woodrow Wilson in cap) was a Wilson supporter and former presidential candidate who earned the coveted post of Secretary of State following Wilson's election in 1912. That election left Democrats in charge of both houses of Congress and the Presidency. Posters on both sides of the Atlantic (opposite page, from Great Britain) urged citizens to support the war effort in memory of victims of the *Lusitania*.

In fact Wilson had carefully avoided combat after the *Lusitania* went down. He tried instead to be a peacemaker for Europe and sought to bring harmony and democracy to the world's citizens. Thus for two years he employed diplomacy and his powers of persuasion to avoid war. For a while he succeeded. Although Germans briefly celebrated the *Lusitania's* sinking, the subsequent condemnation of the act as barbaric and criminal forced the Kaiser to scale back his submarine campaign. In the months that followed, Wilson scolded Germany when it occasionally attacked American-related shipping, and Germany responded by once again avoiding American targets. Even as people like Roosevelt urged for military combat to replace verbal combat, plenty of Americans remained reluctant to shed blood for what was essentially seen as a fight between old-world rivals. These citizens helped reelect Wilson in 1916 with the campaign slogan, "He kept us out of war."

★ **WILSON'S ADVISORS HAD MIXED FEELINGS** about war. His first Secretary of State, William Jennings Bryan, had resigned in protest over Wilson's favoritism toward the British during the early months of the European war. Although some members of his administration counseled against war, others favored the idea. So did an influential acquaintance of Wilson's named Edward M. House. House, a wealthy Texan, had befriended Wilson during his quick rise to power. In the space of three years Wilson had gone from being the president of Princeton University to serving as governor of New Jersey to winning election, in 1912, as President of the United States. House had become one of Wilson's closest and most trusted advisors during this transition and, although he had declined an official role in the government, he remained at the President's service.

In early 1915 House had actually sailed to England on the *Lusitania* to serve there as an informal representative of the President. On the day that *U-boat 20* sank the *Lusitania*, he had predicted at an English dinner party: "We shall be at war with Germany within a month." Although his prediction failed then, House would forecast or promote the idea repeatedly in the months that followed, even as Wilson steadfastly resisted it.

By 1917, though, the President was running out of diplomatic tricks, and Germany's military strategists were despairing on the battlefront. In an effort to regain the chance for victory, the Kaiser declared all-out war on the high seas, regardless of international opinion. German officials gambled that their forces would be able to cripple the Allies' supply lines and defeat their foes before America could declare war, raise an army, train it, and send it into battle. His decision forced Wilson's call to arms.

★ **CONGRESS APPROVED A DECLARATION OF WAR WITHIN DAYS OF** Wilson's April 2nd speech. All but 56 of the 511 votes cast by members of the U.S. House and Senate supported the resolution. Thus a nation that had seen its population swell in recent decades by waves of European immigrants now found itself fighting against the ancestral homelands of some of its newest residents. The prospect loomed for major conflicts in loyalty and allegiance given the fact that a third of the U.S. population had claimed birth on foreign soil for themselves or at least one of their parents during the 1910 census. (President Wilson was one of them; his mother had been born in England.) Many Americans maintained sentimental loyalties, if not outright practical ones, to their motherlands. At that time Germany could claim the greatest number of offspring in America: Perhaps as much as a quarter of the entire U.S. population had either immigrated from Germany or descended from German immigrants.

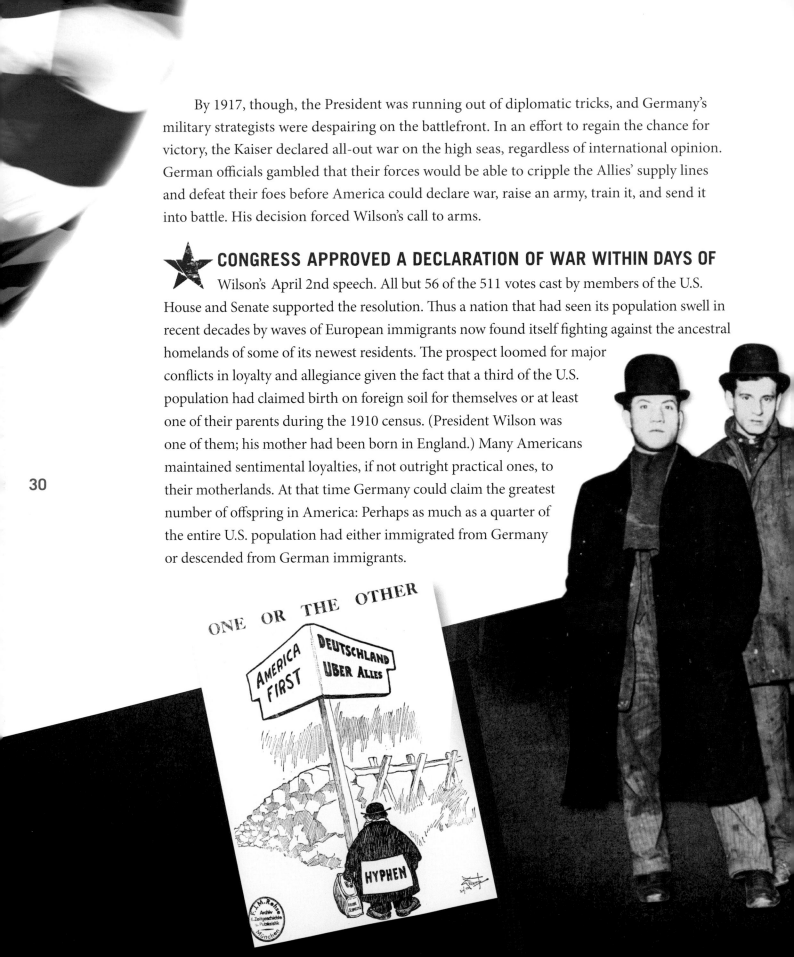

The presence of so many Germans and their descendants assured that German foods and beverages, the German language, German-American clubs and music groups, even bilingual schools, all flourished in the United States prior to World War I. During the early years of the war, while the U.S. government remained on the sidelines of the fight, many German-Americans had felt comfortable offering their public support of the German war effort through speeches, published commentary, and fund-raising. Some ethnic groups, such as the Irish, even cheered for Germany because of their own dislike for Germany's foe, England. Others supported their ancestral homelands.

The divided nature of Americans' old-world loyalties had reinforced Wilson's reluctance to go to war. "We definitely have to be neutral," he is said to have remarked after fighting broke out in Europe, "since otherwise

The hyphens. Americans with hyphenated origins, such as German-Americans, often found their allegiance questioned at the time of World War I (left) even as the vast majority of them took steps to become naturalized citizens (above, 1916 in New York City).

our mixed populations would wage war on each other." President Wilson, still mindful of this concern, had spoken at length during his war message to Congress about the presence of German-Americans in the United States. He clarified that the German government was the nation's true enemy. "We have no quarrel with the German people," he explained. "We have no feelings toward them but one of sympathy and friendship."

Therefore, noted Wilson, Americans should "prove that friendship in our daily attitude and actions towards the millions of men and women of German birth and native sympathy, who live amongst us and share our life. . . . They are, most of them, as true and loyal Americans as if they had never known any other fealty or allegiance." Then Wilson added an ominous warning: "If there should be disloyalty, it will be dealt with with a firm hand of stern repression." Those assembled on April 2 had applauded these words with enthusiasm.

Wilson cautioned his listeners that evening to be mindful of another sort of German, too: "From the very outset of the present war [the German state] has filled our unsuspecting communities and even our offices of government with spies and set criminal intrigues everywhere afoot against our national unity of counsel." Tensions over who could be trusted, whether criticism of the war effort symbolized disloyalty, what it meant to be an American, and whether one could retain connections to a motherland during wartime would dominate the American home front for the rest of the decade. They would touch the lives of citizens as diverse as Eugene Debs, a prominent Socialist and presidential candidate; Victor Berger, a German-American newspaper editor and former member of Congress; and Jane Addams, a peace activist and community organizer in Chicago.

Coast to coast, ordinary citizens going about their everyday lives—from ministers in Texas to miners in Arizona to laborers in Illinois—would soon find their lives upended and changed forever because they lived in a nation at war. The eloquent words of a President may have masked this imminent catastrophe so that it did not offer the visibility of an oncoming missile. But the results of the unfolding crisis would be nearly as shattering to the lives of these Americans as the torpedo had been to those who sailed on the last voyage of the *Lusitania.*

32

German spies? Rumors flew during the run-up to America's entry into World War I that Germany had embedded spies in the U.S. government and elsewhere. Suspicious behavior by two high-profile German officers based in New York at the time of the *Lusitania's* sinking added legitimacy to the stories even though few spies would ever be identified during the war. A playful cartoon (opposite page) depicted the two men—Captain Karl Boy-Ed (left) and Captain Franz Von Papen (below)—as German dachshunds, waiting to be called home.

"To all the disloyal in this country, a message will be **sounded**.... *May God have* **mercy** *on them, for they need expect none from an* **outraged** *people and an* **avenging** *government."*

THOMAS GREGORY, UNITED STATES ATTORNEY GENERAL, NOVEMBER 20, 1917

OFF TO KILL THE HUN

A HUNDRED YEARS AGO—before radio and TV, before wired and wireless messages—public speaking reigned supreme as a means of communication, and gifted orators drew crowds. Thus, on June 16, 1918, when Eugene Debs stepped forward to talk in Canton, Ohio, some 1,200 people were on hand to hear the famous orator speak. One year into the war, the audience recognized that new laws might prevent Debs from saying what was on his mind. Those who gathered wanted to know if the Debs of 1918 was still as fiery as ever.

Revenge.
Artists on both sides of
the Atlantic used posters
to encourage retribution
for the sinking of the
Lusitania (detail from the
illustration for a 1915 British
poster entitled, "Take up the
sword of justice").

Eugene Debs left his listeners with no doubts. The four-time presidential candidate, labor union organizer, and founding member of the Socialist Party of America spoke his mind that day in Canton, as always. He objected to the arrest and imprisonment of three members of the Socialist Party for opposing the war. He observed with irony how "it is extremely dangerous to exercise the constitutional right of free speech in a country fighting to make democracy safe in the world." The outspoken Debs criticized how "the master class has always declared the wars; the subject class has always fought the battles." These business owners then make profits selling arms and supplies, he asserted, while ordinary people fight and die in combat. Debs described American business leaders as "the gentry who are today wrapped up in the American flag . . . eager to apply the brand of treason to the men who dare to whisper their opposition" to this ruling class.

Debs spoke so plainly that, within days, he found himself under arrest for violating the same law that had landed his followers in jail—the Espionage Act of 1917. The Wilson

Administration had proposed the legislation soon after the U.S. declaration of war. The act called for, among other things, the creation of harsh procedures for identifying and detaining spies, penalties for interfering with the war effort, censorship of the news media, and restrictions on the distribution of printed materials through the U.S. mails. The Justice Department had sought similar powers even before Woodrow Wilson's call to arms. Lawmakers who had rejected the earlier requests as too oppressive felt more supportive of them during wartime, a pattern that would repeat itself in the next century with the passage of the privacy-stripping Patriot Act following the 9-11 terrorist attacks of 2001.

★ **THE CALLS FOR THE LEGISLATION GREW OUT OF FEARS REAL AND** imagined. Undoubtedly the waves of immigrants entering the United States during the turn of the century contributed to President Wilson's pointed comments about spies in his April 1917 address. These foreigners hailed from unfamiliar regions such as Eastern Europe and the Mediterranean. They dressed differently, spoke unknown languages, held unfamiliar beliefs, and competed for U.S. jobs. To many long-time residents, these newcomers just didn't seem like real Americans. Could these strange people be trusted? Equally threatening were the German officials who lived in the United States between 1914 and 1917, before America entered the war. Could they be spies? Woodrow Wilson seemed to think so, and so other people did, too. Alleged instances of sabotage and the wartime expulsions from the United States of German representatives like Karl Boy-Ed and Franz Von Papen added credence to this notion even though few other spies were ever identified.

Defining free speech.
President Woodrow Wilson (right) emphasized his patriotism by displaying such symbols as the American flag. Eugene Debs (opposite page) championed the use of less tangible symbols of the nation, such as the constitutional right of free speech. Wilson objected that disloyal Americans "had sacrificed their rights to civil liberties."

Some voices inside and outside Congress questioned the oppressive nature of the bill. "While we are fighting to establish the democracy of the world, we ought not to do the thing that will establish autocracy in America," warned Republican Congressman Martin Madden of Illinois. But others disagreed. "In time of great national peril, it is necessary sometimes that individual citizens shall be willing to surrender some of the privileges which they have for the sake of the greater good," suggested another Republican, Dick Morgan of Oklahoma. Lawmakers did defeat the administration's call for censorship of the press and clarified or softened some other restrictions. Even so, the final provisions gave federal officials sweeping authority to apprehend suspected enemies, stifle criticism of the war effort, and censor the distribution of information through the mails. Within a year, at the administration's request, lawmakers had expanded the government's power to silence its critics even further through what became known as the Sedition Act of 1918. During no war before or since has the United States implemented such harsh legislation.

Eugene Debs was just one of the thousands of Americans who found themselves silenced, harassed, or imprisoned because of the Espionage and Sedition Acts of World War I. Debs defended himself at a trial during the fall of 1918, claiming that the First Amendment to the U.S. Constitution guaranteed his right to freedom of speech. The court disagreed and sentenced Debs to ten years in prison. By the spring of 1919, after losing all appeals, he entered the federal penitentiary in Atlanta, Georgia. At the same time, the government imprisoned a limited

War zone. Conscription, or forced military service, accounted for almost three-fourths of the four million members of U.S. armed forces during World War I. Volunteers made up the rest. By the summer of 1918 some 250,000 soldiers a month entered battlefields in the first conflict to include submarine attacks, aerial combat (above), and chemical warfare.

> "[This act] has all the earmarks of a **dictatorship.** It suppresses free speech and does it all in the name of **war** and **patriotism.**"

WILLIAM EDGAR BORAH, REPUBLICAN SENATOR FROM IDAHO, DURING DEBATE OVER THE ESPIONAGE ACT OF 1917

Master of spin.
George Creel (left) managed a wartime propaganda effort of unprecedented proportions as director of the Committee on Public Information (CPI). American newspapers published ready-made cartoons and news stories prepared by CPI writers and artists. CPI staffers even supplied the nation's ministers with suggested prayers.

Mark of the Hun. Anti-German posters (below) helped motivate Americans to support the war effort through the purchase of Liberty Bonds and through military service. News of horrific casualties on the front—approaching 10 million by war's end—might have undermined support for combat without such propaganda efforts.

Us Bonos de
a Libertad
ayudarán á dar
fin con esto

Your ★ LIBERTY BOND
Will Help Stop This

The Hun~his Mark
Blot it Out
with
LIBERTY
BONDS

Crucified. War support and hatred of the so-called German Hun skyrocketed after rumors began to circulate of German atrocities, including the crucifixion of a Canadian officer on the Belgian front. Propaganda depicted the alleged act (above, a U.S. poster from the Philippines, 1917) even though it turned out to be a false report.

number of enemy aliens, citizens of enemy nations living in the United States who were accused of being a threat to the home front (with or without justification); fewer than 10,000 were detained in comparison to the wholesale incarceration during World War II of 120,000 Japanese-Americans (a majority of whom were U.S. citizens).

At the same time that some officials sought to discourage criticism of the war effort, others worked to stir up patriotic support for the military campaign through the creation of pro-government propaganda. Woodrow Wilson established a special department in 1917 to manage this work and appointed George Creel, a former investigative reporter and presidential campaign worker, to run the Committee on Public Information, or CPI. Creel dove into the task with gusto, intent on creating what he called "the world's greatest adventure in advertising."

Creel's office recruited some 75,000 volunteers to talk up the war effort; these so-called four-minute men (named for their short speeches and in honor of the minute men of Revolutionary War fame) spoke in their own communities at movie theaters and other public gatherings. The CPI produced promotional movies about the war effort. It staged county fair–like displays of U.S. military equipment and of wartime booty captured abroad. It created "war study" course materials for use in public schools and at universities. The CPI even opened offices overseas to distribute posters and copies of Wilson's speeches (translated into the local languages), as well as general propaganda promoting the U.S. war effort.

All of these efforts carried two messages: The positive message encouraged Americans to be patriotic and support the war effort; the more ominous one stoked fears and hatred of the enemy. The twin threads reinforced one another. Concerns about national security made Americans more supportive of calls for military service, more willing to offer financial support to the war, and more cooperative with wartime economies (such as conservation of the food and energy that needed to be diverted to the war effort). Creel's propaganda campaign made citizens more eager to keep a watchful eye on suspicious neighbors or unusual activity, too.

CPI posters and publications portrayed the enemy in brutally graphic terms. Early on in the conflict German leader Kaiser Wilhelm II had compared his nation's forces to the Huns, fierce warriors who overran Europe around 450 A.D. The term stuck, immediately transferring onto the Germans the negative associations of cruelty and ruthlessness that are tied to the reputation of the Huns. Rumors swirled and went unchecked: that German soldiers were torturing civilians caught up in the European invasions, that victorious Germans would invade America, killing civilians with bayonets, and so on. Soon the CPI was creating posters, some dripping with blood-red ink, that urged Americans to rally in the

TWENTY YEARS
AT HULL-HOUSE

JANE ADDAMS

Rejected. Jane Addams (below, above the letter "P," with peace conference delegates) had been called the most-loved woman in the world before the war. Her fame arose from her work as a founder of the settlement house movement that created community-based service centers for urban immigrants. Her 1910 book (left) about Chicago's Hull-House became a national best seller. But during World War I Addams found that not even her immense national reputation could earn her the right to speak out for peace.

PEACE

PEACE DELEGATES ON NOORDAM

fight to defeat the Huns—in other words, Germany. Such rhetoric fed a wave of anti-German sentiment in the United States, most of it directed against innocent immigrants, their descendants, and their German culture.

⭐ AMERICANS RUSHED TO ERADICATE ALL THINGS GERMAN.

Restaurants renamed the signature German dish of sauerkraut liberty cabbage. Hamburgers became liberty steak. Bars stopped serving pretzels. The German measles illness turned into liberty measles. Symphony orchestras and opera houses stopped playing music written by German composers. Schoolteachers cut German songs out of songbooks or pasted new pages over top of them. Businesses, towns, and individuals jettisoned their German-sounding names. The German Savings Bank became the American Savings Bank. Berlin became Belleville. German Street became English Street. Schmidt families turned into Smiths. When Eddie Reichenbacher, a famed World War I American flying ace, respelled his name as Eddie Rickenbacker, newspapers proclaimed that he had "taken the Hun out of his name!" Even serious matters, such as establishing a national health insurance plan, lost favor because the idea was based on a German model.

CPI propaganda efforts aroused fears about other foreigners, too, such as the Russian immigrants and other radicals who supported the Socialist Party. Even well-regarded American citizens came under attack as pressure mounted for all criticism of the government and its war effort to cease. College professors were encouraged to keep quiet rather than voice dissenting opinions. Women who campaigned for their own democratic right to vote by staging protests at the White House were attacked and arrested. Politicians who questioned government practices were condemned as un-American. Anyone who criticized the government could be silenced with the charge that, since they were against the government, they must be pro-German or a radical; both were deadly stigmas to bear.

Rebukes weren't limited to truly radical figures like Eugene Debs. When the popular social reformer Jane Addams defended her right to talk about peace, even during wartime, she watched her national stature crumble. Women who had supported her earlier efforts on behalf of international peace now refused to listen. Audiences booed her. Groups cancelled plans to have her speak. "Jane Addams is losing her grip," objected a reporter for a woman's club newspaper. "She is becoming a bore." The Daughters of the American Revolution even voted to throw her out of their organization after the war. In an effort to demonstrate its patriotism, the nation cast aside its most famous heroine. The pre-war influence of Jane Addams and other such figures who questioned current events vanished just as completely as if it had sunk beneath the ocean waves with the *Lusitania*.

43

Uncle Sam. Artist James Montgomery Flagg created his icon of patriotism in 1916 for *Leslie's* newspaper. Later he drew for George Creel at the CPI. In 1917 Flagg's Uncle Sam (here, promoting Liberty Bonds) spoke for the first time the now-famous military recruitment line: "I Want YOU!"

"In times of war people grow hysterical, *and when* people grow *hysterical even executives, even legislative bodies, are* not exempt *from the contagion of hysteria."*

THOMAS HARDWICK, DEMOCRATIC SENATOR FROM GEORGIA, APRIL 5, 1918

HOLD YOUR TONGUE

ROBERT PRAGER, A COAL MINER** from southern Illinois, had three strikes against him during the First World War. For starters, he was a German immigrant. Second, he was a socialist. The third strike? Other miners worried that Prager was a spy (even though he was not). On April 5, 1918, after an evening of drinking, three of Prager's coworkers set out to confront him. The men found Prager, stripped off his outer clothes, wrapped him in an American flag, and escorted him through town. A mob of curious onlookers marched with the prisoner and his captors out into the countryside. Next they watched as the men tied one end of a rope around a high tree limb and the other around Prager's neck. Then, to express their patriotism, his executioners dropped Robert Prager's body three times, "one for the red, one for the white, and one for the blue."

The lynching of Robert Prager fit within a pattern of vigilante violence that took place on the home front during World War I. Government officials had ignited the mob rule by asking citizens to help authorities root out spies and enemies. When George Creel of the CPI suggested that patriots establish quasi-official law enforcement groups, organizations sprang up across the nation. The American Protective League, for example, signed up more than 250,000 members. Other groups formed with names like the Boy Spies of America and the Terrible Threateners. Public figures added partisan fuel to the flames, including former Republican President Theodore Roosevelt, who characterized ethnic German-Americans as "not Americans at all, but traitors to America and tools and servants of Germany." With such a backdrop, the overzealous stepped from detective and spy to judge and executioner. By the end of the war more than 70 Americans had died at the hands of vigilantes.

★ MANY CITIZEN ORGANIZATIONS FOCUSED ON SELLING LIBERTY

Bonds, a fund-raising device that helped pay for the war effort. Even though contributions were voluntary, those people who declined to buy bonds risked suspicion as German sympathizers or worse. Citizen groups shamed non-supporters by posting their names in public. Some communities seized people's property and sold it in order to purchase Liberty Bonds for them. Store clerks in Ohio abducted a non-compliant co-worker, wrapped her in an American flag, and dragged her to her bank where they forced her to withdraw money to pay for a bond. A retired minister in Oklahoma who was critical of Liberty Bonds found himself being painted with hot tar then coated with feathers, a painful and humiliating punishment that originated in the Middle Ages. Others found themselves painted yellow, were forced to kiss the American flag, or had their hair cut off.

Although German-Americans received the brunt of scrutiny and punishment, plenty of suspicion was leveled at other groups who seemed to question the American government or threaten current practices of American life. Socialists who advocated for worker rights through the protection of labor unions became popular targets.

"UNANIMOUSLY LOYAL"

F. J. M. Rehse
Archiv
f. Zeitgeschichte
u. Publizistik
München

GERMAN

GERMANY
IS
RIGHT

LANGUAGE

GERMANY
IS
RIGHT

NEWSPAPERS

GERMANY
IS
RIGHT

German *and* American. For decades German-Americans celebrated both sides of their hyphenated heritage: "Germany my mother; America my bride," they proclaimed. But the start of World War I made old-stock Americans question everything German-American, from breweries (below, workers pose circa 1900 outside Wisconsin's Potosi Brewery) to newspapers (left, a cartoonist accuses America's German-language newspapers of publishing stories with a bias in favor of the motherland).

12. Have you ever been naturalized, partly or wholly, in any country other than the United States? *No* If yes, state when and where and in what country _____ ("Yes" or "No.")

13. Has your present husband ever applied for naturalization in or taken out first papers of naturalization in the United States? _____ ("Yes" or "No.") If yes, state when and where _____

14. Has your present husband ever been naturalized, either wholly or partly, in any country other than the United States? *No* ("Yes" or "No.") If yes, state when and where and in what country _____

15. Have you ever taken an oath of allegiance to any country, State, or nation other than the United States? *No* If yes, state when, where, and on ("Yes" or "No.") Are you on parole? ("Yes" or "No.") what charge _____

16. Have you ever been arrested or detained on any charge? *No* If yes, state number of permit ("Yes" or "No.")

17. Have you a permit to enter forbidden areas? *No* If yes, state number of permit _____

(18) Languages:
Spoken *German, English, Latin*
Written *German, English, Latin*
Read *German, English, Latin*

I solemnly swear that all the above statements and answers by me made are true.
Josephine Weissenberger (Signature.)

Sworn to before me this *25th* day of *June*, 19*18*.
at *Atchison, Kans. Police Dept.*
F. C. Snyder (Registration officer.)
Chief of Police
(Official title, office, or post office or other title.)

Left thumb print, if registrant can not write.

DESCRIPTION OF REGISTRANT.
(To be filled in by registration officer.)

Age *28* years *3* months. Mouth *large*
Height *5 ft. 2 in.* Chin *round*
Weight *125 lb.* Hair *darkbrown*
Forehead *medium* Complexion *fair*
Eyes *blue* Face *oval*
Nose *normal*
Distinctive marks. *crippled finger*
Name *Sr Mary Opportuna O.S.B.*
Address *Atchison, Kansas*

Sister Mary Opportuna O.S.B.

48

Alien invaders! Wartime measures required all German immigrants over the age of 14 to be fingerprinted, complete a questionnaire (left, a sample page), and swear allegiance to the United States. Nearly 500,000 German-born citizens complied. The *Bisbee Daily Review* praised Arizona vigilantes for their "display of patriotism and high-minded public spirit" in the roundup (below) of striking copper-mine workers. The local sheriff described the strikers as "those strange men who have congregated here from other parts."

Marching from Dep... Ju...

Demands that had seemed merely radical before the war were viewed as downright un-American during it. Thus the war effort became a convenient excuse for suppressing the development of organized labor.

In Bisbee, Arizona, local citizens took matters into their own hands when workers walked off their copper-mining jobs in June of 1917 with demands to unionize, war or no war. Harry Wheeler, the local sheriff, deputized thousands of volunteers and private detectives to break the strike. During early-morning raids on July 12 they rounded up some 1,200 workers, herded them at gunpoint into manure-coated cattle cars, shipped them across state lines, and dumped them in a desert town with orders not to return. The operation left one striker and one raider dead; all strikes ceased. In the following months, Wheeler and his deputies enforced a lockdown on Bisbee, setting their own rules, issuing their own identification passes, restricting freedom of movement, and subjecting residents to loyalty tests. Individuals who failed the tests were forced to work on prison gangs at the copper mine. "Perhaps everything I did wasn't legal," Wheeler admitted after state and federal authorities stepped in later that year, but his actions went unpunished.

Voluntary policing groups enforced their own ideas about censorship, too. Citizens in more than one community in the United States cleared German-language books off their library shelves and set them on fire. Such occasions might take on a festive atmosphere with band music, singing, and speeches. Other communities acted with more restraint and simply sold the books for scrap. Scorned schools and churches were burned to the ground. Citizen-organized defense societies imposed language restrictions on local citizens, such as one in Grant County, Oklahoma, that forbade telephone operators to connect calls for people who spoke in German.

Other groups served as spies and snitches, for example routing out "slackers," the nickname for people who tried to avoid registering for service in the military. Reports of enemy behavior poured into the Justice Department in Washington, D.C., at the rate of 1,000 or more notices a day. Not one of these leads produced any actual spies. An investigator following up on a tip in Centralia, Washington, for example, learned that an alleged German spy had been turned in by none other than a "Miss Brundage [who] proved to be a member of the seventh grade of the primary schools and but 13 years of age." By the end of the war, the Espionage Act of 1917 had netted exactly zero spies.

Devil dogs. U.S. Marines trace the origin of their nickname, the devil dogs, to World War I, claiming that their persistence in battle against German fighters earned them that name of respect. Such symbolism played out in political cartoons of the era (right, a "Teufel Hunden" or, roughly translated, "devil dog" pursues a retreating German dachshund across the Marne River of France).

50

with Apologies to a
U.S. MARINE POSTER

"TEUFEL HUNDEN" ON THE MARNE

Those spared the nooses of the vigilantes found their fates at risk in the nation's courts. Judges scrambled to interpret new laws and weigh their intent against protections like the First Amendment right of free speech as set out in the U.S. Constitution, all within a context of wartime hysteria. Many of the accused encountered judges and juries who supported the new restrictive laws. A patron at a bar in Illinois found himself sentenced to two years at the notorious Fort Leavenworth prison for commenting that Germany was "all right." Three men who left a tavern singing a German war song earned six months of labor at a workhouse. A Russian-American woman speaking to a women's club received a ten-year sentence for suggesting that the nation's war effort was designed to benefit the corporations that made military weapons. (Some of these extreme sentences were shortened after the war.)

WOODROW WILSON KEPT TO THE SIDELINES WHILE MANY of these home-front developments unfolded. Although he encouraged members of his administration to show restraint in their prosecutions, he rarely overruled them, preferring instead to focus his attention on plans for the postwar peace. While Wilson looked the other way, hundreds of government workers under the leadership of A. Mitchell Palmer, the wartime alien property custodian, systematically seized the assets of German-Americans, claiming that the owners had ties to the enemy. The sizeable German-American brewing industry became a favorite target at a time when anti-German sentiments fanned support for the prohibition of the sale of alcoholic beverages. Within a year Palmer, a future attorney general, and his staff had confiscated some $700 million worth of German-American property.

The execution of Robert Prager did draw comments from President Wilson, although his concerns arose more out of frustration at the way Germany had exploited the attack in its own propaganda. "Every American who takes part in the action of a mob or gives it any sort of countenance is no true son of this great Democracy," Wilson asserted. But the momentum of citizen-based policing and vigilante justice had taken hold on wartime America, and periodic calls for restraint by President Wilson and Attorney General Thomas Gregory did nothing to halt the movement.

Citizens gathered in Omaha, Nebraska, at a stein-breaking festival to destroy the distinctive German beer mugs. Officials locked up the German-born conductor of the Boston Symphony Orchestra under charges of being an enemy alien. And residents of Columbus, Ohio, reportedly put to death local dogs from German breeds, such as dachshunds. However, these isolated incidents could not match the systematic destruction underway in the country of the use of German in American schools.

Until World War I, German-language instruction had dominated the language education scene in the United States, from elementary schools through universities. German served as the international language for scientists and other academic intellectuals. Many public schools anchored their programs with bilingual instruction in English and German, particularly in regions with strong German immigrant populations. Bilingual programs served both native speakers and children who would otherwise have had no contact with German. They featured not only German-language classes but also classes taught in German for other academic subjects, such as math or science. At the high school and college levels, German eclipsed all other foreign languages as the language of choice. In 1915, nearly half of all public and private high schools offered foreign language instruction. German students outnumbered those studying French by almost three to one. Spanish enrollments came in a distant third behind the other two options.

Such patterns evaporated after 1917 even though government officials suggested no change was required. "The United States is now at war with the imperial government of Germany and not with the German language or literature," advised the U.S. Commissioner of Education in 1917. Nonetheless, when the United States went to war against Germany in Europe, American citizens went to war against the German language on the home front. Local communities and states raced to pass laws restricting the use of German in their schools. The sentiments expressed in an American Defense Society brochure reflected a common public opinion: German "is not a fit language to teach clean and pure American boys and girls."

Whereas 14 states at the turn of the century had required that academic instruction take place only in English, 35 states had adopted that position by the early 1920s. By then almost half of the states forbade the teaching of any foreign language to elementary school children. Many states specifically outlawed the teaching of German at any level. Some laws even applied to private and church-run schools. Even where German-language instruction continued to be available, such as at American colleges and universities, German-language enrollments plummeted as students opted to take different foreign languages. In the space of two academic years at the University of Wisconsin, for example, German-language enrollments fell from 1,400 students at the beginning of the 1916 school year to 180 students by the fall of 1918.

Some of these changes followed the natural progression that came from the maturing of the German-American population as fewer Germans immigrated to the United States and those here became more integrated into American culture. But the anti-German sentiments of the period hastened this shift. Much of the harshest criticism fell on the language teachers themselves, who were often accused of being supporters of the German war effort simply because they taught the German language. Many lost their jobs, either as punishment for pre-war statements of support for Germany or because their classrooms had been emptied by anti-German legislation and sentiment.

When state and local governments felt federal guidelines were not strict enough, they passed laws of their own. The school district of Los Angeles, for example, outlawed classroom discussions on the merits of peace. State and local governments banned the use of German beyond the classroom, too—from places of business to houses of worship to the sidewalks of America's main streets. Local residents who defied the bans might be arrested or attacked. For example, a Lutheran minister in Texas earned a whipping after defying a local vigilante group and delivering a sermon in German. Other behaviors deemed un-American drew harsh reactions, too. An outspoken history professor near an army recruiting station in New York City was sent to the

"*The gospel of* hate *is not a necessary spur to make America fight.... This foe of* modern times *must be overcome. But ... it can be done without resorting to the* debasing tactics *of Germany herself.*"

EDITORIAL WRITER, *NORTHWESTERN CHRISTIAN ADVOCATE*, FALL 1918

53

Ashes and smoke.

In the space of a generation, German-Americans who could proudly stand in front of their ethnic stores (central image, 1896, scene from Sheboygan, Wisconsin) literally saw their heritage go up in smoke once the U.S. joined the First World War. In Baraboo, Wisconsin, after the school board voted to remove German from the local curriculum, students spirited away the high school's German-language books on a June evening in 1918 and set them on fire (inset image). They painted an eerie epitaph beside the ashes: "Here lies the remains of German in B.H.S."

54

Hold that mail. "The bureaucrats of the Post Office Department . . . seem determined to set up an intellectual reign of terror in the U.S.," observed the *New York World* in the fall of 1918. Postmaster General Albert Burleson (right) led that effort, making Victor Berger (above), the German-American editor of the *Milwaukee Leader,* a target of close scrutiny. President Woodrow Wilson urged restraint but only overruled Burleson's judgments on two occasions; both involved English-language periodicals.

local mental institution for the evaluation of his sanity. A theater patron in Pittsburgh found himself arrested, jailed, and fined for refusing to stand during the playing of the national anthem.

★ THE ESPIONAGE ACT OF 1917 ASSURED THAT NEWSPAPERS AND

magazines faced similar restrictions. Albert Burleson, as Postmaster General for the Wilson Administration, strictly enforced the act's non-mailability provision. This legislation gave him the authority to revoke the postage rights of newspapers and other periodicals that appeared to threaten the war effort. In an era when print media served as the main means for spreading news, and the mails served as a central way to transport them, the loss of access to distribution through the U.S. mails provided a potential death sentence for a publication. Publications written in the German language suffered the most; more than half of them—a total of some 320 periodicals—went out of business during the war. Even English-language publications risked closure. Editors found themselves threatened with charges of treason just for publishing articles that questioned the war effort.

Periodicals that supported the Socialist Party were a favorite target, too, whether they were published in English or German. Victor Berger, editor of the pro-Socialist *Milwaukee Leader*, provoked Burleson's wrath by publishing anti-war editorials. Berger, who had helped found the Socialist Party with Eugene Debs, had, in 1910, been the first Socialist to win election to Congress. During 1917 and 1918 the Postmaster General charged Berger on three occasions with violating the Espionage Act, and he revoked his access to the U.S. mails. Berger lost his case and was sentenced in 1918 to 20 years in prison, pending an appeal.

Even in the absence of direct force, a sense of oppression hung in the air. Plenty of people acted the part of being patriotic out of fear that they could be the next person wrapped in a flag and marched off to buy a Liberty Bond, the next person punished for speaking a foreign language, the next person hanged from a tree as a traitor. German-Americans volunteered to serve in the military. Some offered their services as informants and translators. Immigrants waved American flags at parades. German-American music groups and other organizations disbanded, with some donating leftover club funds to the Red Cross as further proof of their patriotism. Children of immigrants rushed to learn English. Older immigrants retreated to their homes when they wanted to speak German. Just as children might be urged to "hold your tongue" around grown-ups, immigrants learned not to use their native languages. Some maintained an eerie silence, refusing to speak at all.

H. L. Mencken, a noted writer and social commentator of the time, summed up the home-front scene with these words: "Between Wilson and his brigades of informers, spies, volunteer detectives, perjurers and complaisant judges . . . the liberty of the citizens has pretty well vanished in America."

"Any man who resists the present tides *that run in the world will find himself thrown upon a shore so* high *and* barren *that it will seem as if he had been* separated *from his* human kind *forever."*

WOODROW WILSON, FEBRUARY 24, 1919

BETWEEN WAR AND PEACE

BY 1918, THE UNITED STATES found itself at war on three fronts: on the battlefields of Europe, in the hometowns of America, and within the chambers of the country's judicial system. Surely when Woodrow Wilson issued his eloquent call in 1917 to make the world safe for democracy, the President never anticipated that some of the greatest battles of that fight would take place just a few blocks away from the White House at meetings of the United States Supreme Court.

Mobilized.
"I see no reason why one should not say what one believes in time of war as in time of peace," Jane Addams suggested in 1917. Americans debated the home-front right to speak freely during wartime even as troops fought for democracy abroad.

Prior to World War I, the Supreme Court had given little consideration to the right of free speech. Until then, few court cases had questioned how to interpret the intent of the Constitution's First Amendment as set forth in the Bill of Rights. All of that changed after 1917. Suddenly people were arguing all the time about who had the right to speak, what they could be prevented from saying, and whether new laws such as the Espionage and Sedition Acts overstepped the protections of free speech as guaranteed by the First Amendment. These debates worked their way through the lower courts until key cases began to reach the U.S. Supreme Court with appeals for further review. Beginning in 1919 the nine-man court considered the arguments of the day.

In its earliest wartime rulings—three separate cases involving wartime critics named Schenck, Frowherk, and Debs—the Supreme Court sided with authorities who had silenced these voices of dissent. In the case of Eugene Debs, for example, the judges agreed unanimously in 1919 that his imprisonment was justified. But, within months of these initial rulings, two of the court's judges began to rethink the issue. Oliver Wendell Holmes and Louis Brandeis began to argue for a broader interpretation of First Amendment rights. A series of split court decisions followed, with Holmes and Brandeis opposing the prevailing opinion that speech could be restricted, especially during wartime.

Even as the legal battles at home heated up, the fever pitch of combat in Europe began to wind down. By the end of the summer of 1918, the Germans had lost their 1917 gamble of overpowering the enemy with all-out submarine warfare. Their own resources and strength were running out just as endless waves of American troops arrived to reinforce the Allied offensive. On November 9, 1918, Kaiser Wilhelm II abdicated, or abandoned, his rule over Germany. Two days later, all fighting stopped on what became known as Armistice Day. "A supreme moment of history has come," proclaimed Woodrow Wilson. "The hand of God is laid upon the nations."

★ SUCH LANGUAGE CAME NATURALLY TO WILSON, THE SON OF

a Presbyterian minister. As a devout Christian, Wilson had populated his cabinet with religious men and infused his foreign policy with their religious convictions. He saw God's hand behind the victory in Europe, and he felt called by God to assure that the war led to lasting peace. Thus, at a time when no President had ever before left the country while in office, Wilson insisted that he personally represent the United States at treaty negotiations in France; no one else could be trusted to execute his lofty expectations, he felt. This decision placed him an ocean away from the seat of government at a time when the nature of travel and communication left him

GERMANY SURRENDERS

WE WANT DEBS

Peace and war.

Although fighting stopped in Europe in November 1918 (above, New Yorkers celebrate the news), controversy and conflicts remained in full swing on the American home front. Nonetheless Woodrow Wilson remained focused on Europe and postwar peace negotiations. In 1920 Eugene Debs, still in prison (right) for his anti-war criticisms, campaigned with the slogan, "For President—Convict # 9653." He earned nearly a million votes, almost as many as he had received in his 1912 bid (far right, a button from an earlier Debs campaign).

virtually cut off from the nation's capital. With the exception of one brief return visit to the U.S., Wilson remained abroad from early December 1918 to early July 1919.

Wilson left town with a crumbling political base thanks to midterm elections that had allowed Republicans to seize control of both houses of Congress. Those Democrats who remained in office lacked strong leadership. Some Socialists were victorious in 1918, too. Eugene Debs won a seat in the House of Representatives that he would be unable to fill because he remained in jail; Victor Berger, though victorious in the voting booth and free on appeal, found himself barred from taking his seat by a vote of his House colleagues. Even though voters chose him again during a 1919 special election for his vacant post, House members still refused to seat him in early 1920 because of his pending court case.

The President's foreign absence and unwavering focus on international affairs came during deepening troubles on the American home front. African Americans who had migrated north in search of better living standards and the promise of wartime jobs found themselves increasingly unwelcome. A 1917 race riot in East St. Louis left scores dead and prompted protesters to march through New York City carrying such signs as

Persona non grata. Foreign nationals who found themselves in the spotlight during wartime (above right, a multilingual notice from 1917) remained there through the uneasy transition that followed World War I. The deportation of such *persona non grata* as unwanted aliens (right, deporting Germans) began with the passage of the Alien Act of 1918. Nearly 12,000 aliens found themselves deported in just the first year of the act's enforcement.

"Mr. President, Why Not Make AMERICA Safe for Democracy?" and "Bring Democracy to America Before You Carry It to Europe." Other race riots broke out during 1918 and 1919 in such cities as Philadelphia, Chicago, and Washington, D.C. The return of American soldiers added further pressure to the situation, with whites competing against blacks for their pre-war jobs.

The war had fueled other domestic issues, too. Hostility toward the German-American-dominated brewing industry contributed to passage of a so-called prohibition amendment to the U.S. Constitution, banning the sale of alcohol in the U.S. after 1919. The war had also prompted women to become increasingly insistent that a nation fighting for democracy abroad owed its own female citizens the right to vote at home. Lest Wilson overlook their point, a group of volunteers began staging protests in front of the White House in 1917; in 1919 they were still at it. Other domestic issues included postwar inflation and a worldwide flu epidemic that killed half- a-million Americans during 1918 and 1919.

62

Contrarian rival. Henry Cabot Lodge (left), a powerful Republican senator from Massachusetts who had frequently criticized the Democratic Wilson during his Presidency, questioned the soundness of Wilson's push for a postwar League of Nations. Lodge worried that U.S. participation in the peacekeeping League would undercut America's independence, concluding that the U.S. might be forced to follow League decisions—such as going to war—even if its leaders opposed them.

MEANWHILE AUTHORITIES FRESH FROM HUNTING FOR GERMAN spies intensified their scrutiny of labor leaders with ties to socialism and other non-mainstream political beliefs. J. Edgar Hoover, the man whose name would eventually become synonymous with the Federal Bureau of Investigation (FBI), organized the effort from a small office within President Wilson's Justice Department. His investigators targeted the so-called radicals who were fighting against American industrial powers for the rights of workers to form unions and improve their employment conditions. The department's effort became known as the Red Scare because of charges that these labor organizers were tied to the red-flag-bearing revolutionaries of the World War I era who had taken over Russia and established communist rule in the new Soviet Union.

Identifying local labor organizers proved easier to do than the earlier assignment of finding German spies. Using the provisions of a companion bill, the Alien Act of 1918, authorities rounded up hundreds of Americans, even citizens, and deported them to countries they may have immigrated from decades earlier. Few of those deported posed any actual threat to the U.S. government, and their expulsion was soon regarded as an overreaction to exaggerated fears.

Home-front tensions mattered little to a President who felt that he had a God-given duty to make World War I the "War to End all Wars," in a popular phrase of the day. Wilson told Congress that securing world peace would repay the war's dead by "making good what they offered their life's blood to obtain." Wilson had identified a list of 14 points that he hoped would form the basis of the peace treaty. Creating a peacekeeping League of Nations remained one of his personal favorites. He envisioned that a league, made up of representatives of all major powers, could team up against offending members and discourage them from behaving in aggressive or dangerous ways.

Because of his help during the war and his commitment to worldwide peace, Woodrow Wilson received a hero's welcome when he arrived in Europe. "He ceased to be a common statesman," observed the writer H. G. Wells. "He became a Messiah." Two million people lined the streets to welcome him in Paris. Crowds cheered him in England and Italy. Newspapers dubbed him "The Moses from Across the Atlantic." Yet peace talks proved problematic. Victorious Europeans argued for territorial gains and financial reimbursements at Germany's expense, while the American delegation proved to be better at making grand statements than negotiating. As an example, Edward House undid early agreements when he took Wilson's place in Paris while the President made his brief detour back to the United States. Health challenges further complicated the deliberations as negotiators, including Wilson, became ill from the flu epidemic or other ailments.

"I have found one can **never** *get anything in this world that is* **worthwhile** *without* **fighting** *for it."*

WOODROW WILSON TO EDWARD HOUSE,
JUNE 1919, AS WILSON PREPARES FOR THE
PEACE TREATY RATIFICATION FIGHT

On a mission. "The spirit of the crowd seemed at times akin to fanaticism," reported the *New York Times* during a stop on Woodrow Wilson's cross-country League of Nations tour in 1919 (below, 50,000 people rally in San Diego, California). Wilson visited 10 states and delivered 32 major addresses in 22 days before collapsing from exhaustion. First Lady Edith Wilson (right, with the President) stepped in to manage his affairs as her husband's health deteriorated.

50,000
Greeting
at St
San Diego

Even after Wilson returned to the United States, he remained distracted from home-front issues. Instead he focused his attention on ratification by the U.S. Senate of what became known as the Versailles Treaty from the European peace conference. Such approval might have been straightforward when Democrats controlled Congress, but now, with Republicans in charge, Wilson faced a tougher sell. He spent the rest of the summer pushing lawmakers to support his prized treaty, refusing to compromise as concerns arose over the powers being granted to the League of Nations.

When support for the treaty lagged on Capitol Hill, Wilson embarked on an ambitious cross-country speaking tour to recruit public pressure for its passage. Although his fame drew enthusiastic crowds, the tour failed to help the treaty. Instead, the exertion of travel and public speaking nearly killed the President. After collapsing from exhaustion during the homebound journey, Wilson was rushed back to the White House. Within days, he experienced a major stroke that left him mentally challenged and physically disabled for the rest of his life.

During an era before constant and invasive news coverage, the President's wife and closest advisors conspired to keep secret the seriousness of Wilson's illness. Their efforts were motivated by their sense of loyalty to the President and their desire to protect his health and his reputation. Their key objective was to avoid his

forced retirement from office prior to the ending of his term in March of 1921. Edith Wilson, with the support of the President's personal physician and Joseph Tumulty, his personal secretary, began screening all correspondence directed to the President and determining what matters should be brought to his attention.

The nation's business limped along with the continued absence of Wilson's full engagement. People rarely ever saw the President, not even members of his own cabinet. Those few who did were uniformly shocked. Wilson was "sicker than the world ever knew, and never afterwards was he more than a shadow of his former self," observed a long-time member of the White House staff. "Even when conscious, he was unreasonable, unnatural, simply impossible." Robert Lansing, Wilson's Secretary of State, resigned from office rather than take part in the secret circle of power around the President. "If it ever gets out it will make a fine scandal," he observed in December 1919.

Near the end of Wilson's term of office, the U.S. Senate held two votes on ratification of the Versailles Treaty. Both resulted in defeat. So did the election of 1920, from the standpoint of Democrats, who lost the Presidency to Republican Warren G. Harding. Republicans added significantly to their control of Congress, too, by reaching out to German-Americans and others who had suffered during the war and earning their votes.

As the nation transitioned from wartime to peace, the excesses of home-front repression began to fade. Cooler heads and more moderate voices rose to condemn the repressive tactics of the Red Scare. Such criticism led to the ending of the program

Changing of the guard.
Woodrow Wilson left office in 1921 with his health broken and his dream for a League of Nations unfulfilled (left, looking frail at his final cabinet meeting). American service members who came home during the final months of his administration did not necessarily return empty-handed; some introduced new German immigrants to the American home front (far left, three German brides in transit to America with their soldier husbands and babies).

and may have helped to initiate the shift toward freedom of speech and other civil liberties that began soon after among members of the U.S. Supreme Court. Yet, fear-based restrictions on civil liberties resurfaced in later decades, for example during the Cold War when the nation became concerned again about the influence of the Soviet Union on American society. In each case, these reactions developed at times when the nation was experiencing rapid change, such as with the influx of immigrants or shifts in the makeup of the nation's workforce. Those who felt most threatened by such changes often became the most committed critics and organizers against them, insisting that only they could represent true American morals and values.

Woodrow Wilson left office on March 4, 1921, as Americans continued to heal the fissures that had opened on the home front during the recent war. With his health and reputation in tatters, few could have predicted, even after his receipt of a Nobel Peace Prize in 1920, that his name would ever regain the regard and respect of earlier days.

"If there is any **moral** to be drawn from this historical review it is that suspension of the Bill of Rights, even in the face of **emergency,** is neither necessary nor wise."

HENRY STEELE COMMAGER, HISTORIAN, 1939

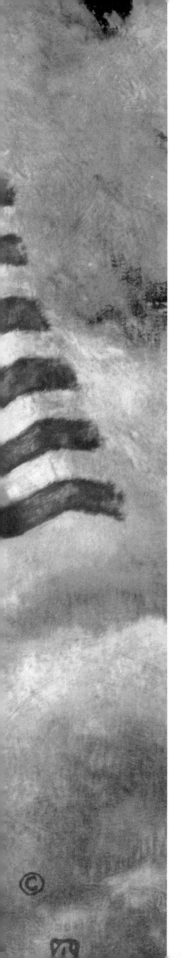

AFTERWORD

WHEN WORLD WAR I ENDED, life in the United States did not

go back to how it had been in the days before the sinking of the

Lusitania. Things were different, and they stayed that way. The U.S.

government had matured into a professional bureaucracy

that collected income taxes, maintained a standing military force,

managed the admission of immigrants to its shores, and, when it

wanted to, spied on its residents in the name of national defense.

The examination of First Amendment rights that had begun during the

war continued until, by the late 1920s, a majority of Supreme Court

justices began to agree with Oliver Wendell Holmes and Louis Brandeis that citizens had a broader right to free speech than the judges had originally thought. The court added further protections to the constitutional right to free speech in the decades that followed. Organizations that saw their birth during the First World War—such as the American Civil Liberties Union—went on to mature after the conflict into major advocates for civil rights.

Even as legislators argued in 1919 about the ratification of the Treaty of Versailles, they agreed after years of debate and delay to amend the U.S. Constitution so that women would have the right to vote in national elections; supporters secured ratification of the 19th Amendment in time for women to participate in the presidential election of 1920. By then the 18th Amendment, banning the sale of alcoholic beverages, had already taken effect. This program of prohibition, as it was called, proved to be short-lived. By 1933 Congress and the states had voted to repeal it.

The War to End All Wars concluded officially for Americans in 1921 following the signing of a separate peace treaty between the U.S. and Germany. By then the Versailles Treaty had taken effect without America's support, and other countries were busy organizing a League of Nations without the participation of the United States. Although Congress repealed the Sedition Act in 1920, no such vote occurred for the Espionage Act and, technically, it remains a valid law today.

Woodrow Wilson, at the encouragement of his Justice Department staff, issued pardons as he left office in 1921 so that hundreds of people imprisoned during the war could be set free. Eugene Debs, his one-time presidential rival, was not among them. Wilson specifically overruled the suggestion that Debs be released from jail, perhaps believing that such a public critic of the war should be kept silent while the country honored those who had fought in it. Wilson's successor, Warren G. Harding, pardoned the aging Socialist on Christmas Day, 1921. By then Debs was 66 years old and in failing health. The labor leader turned politician died five years later in 1926.

In 1923 the Supreme Court ruled that it had been illegal to outlaw the teaching of German during the war. Even so, German-language instruction never recovered its pre-war popularity. By 1949, less than one percent of all high school students studied it. Fewer students learned any foreign languages, too. That same year, only 14 percent of all high school students studied either French, Spanish, or German. In 1915 twice that percentage had studied German alone. As the century progressed, English gained favor as an international common language, expanding into geographic and academic areas once dominated by German.

Woodrow and Edith Wilson retired to a home in Washington, D.C. Wilson never recovered his health and grew increasingly feeble in the years following his Presidency. His reputation stayed tarnished for the rest of his life. Armistice Day remained significant to him personally and to the nation. Eventually it was renamed Veteran's Day to honor soldiers from all wars. Wilson managed to outlive his successor (Harding died unexpectedly in August 1923), but when he tried to attend Harding's funeral he could not muster the strength to climb out of his car. Wilson died a few months later, on February 3, 1924, at the age of 67. Edith Wilson lived nearly 40 more years, dying in 1961 at age 89. Historians continue to criticize her directive role in the final months of her husband's administration.

Life carried on for key figures from the war era as the decades unfolded. Edward House,

71

The horrors of war.
Events from World War I, such as the destruction of the *Lusitania* and the development of aerial combat and chemical weapons, forced people to expand their concept of warfare. This shifting reality led World War II commanders to undertake attacks on civilian targets—from Germany's bombing blitz over England (left, refugees in Liverpool), to America's destruction of two major Japanese cities with atomic bombs.

although he fell out of Wilson's favor during peace negotiations in Paris, played a tangential part in politics until his death in 1938. Victor Berger's wartime editorials earned the approval of the U.S. Supreme Court in 1921 when it overturned his earlier convictions. When Berger won election to the House of Representatives in 1922, no one disputed his right to serve. He died in 1929, several months after leaving Congress. The reputation of Jane Addams remained sullied through most of the 1920s. Nonetheless she tirelessly promoted world peace through the organization she had helped found, the Women's International League for Peace and Freedom. Her efforts earned her a Nobel Peace Prize in 1931, the same distinction Wilson had received near the end of his presidency. She died in 1935.

In November 1916, *U-boat 20* ran aground off the coast of Denmark. Unable to free the boat, Captain Walther Schwieger evacuated it and blew it up. The following September, he and his crew went missing while piloting a different submarine, perhaps victims of an underwater minefield. Captain William Turner of the *Lusitania* served out the rest of the war with the Cunard Line. He retired in 1919 at the age of 63 and died 14 years later. *Lusitania* shipboard lovers Gerda Nielson and John Welsh married one another within days of their rescue. Twelve-year-old Avis Dolphin and her life jacket helper Ian Holbourn maintained a friendship that lasted until the professor's death in 1933. The wreck of the *Lusitania* lay undisturbed some 300 feet beneath the Irish Sea until divers began visiting it in 1935. Among the most notable expeditions since then was the exploration undertaken in 1993 by Robert Ballard; his research helped confirm the theory that coal dust had caused the secondary explosions onboard the ship.

The passage of time—and events such as the outbreak of the Second World War in 1939—revitalized Woodrow Wilson's reputation in the decades following his death. Wilson had predicted that another war would follow the Great War if the U.S. failed to join the League. "There will come a time, in the vengeful Providence of God, another struggle in which not a few hundred thousand fine men from America will have to die, but as many millions as are necessary to accomplish the final freedom of the peoples of the world," he suggested during his 1919 speaking tour.

It would fall on the shoulders of President Franklin D. Roosevelt to lead the United States during the next world war. Although his administration avoided many of the home-front mistakes made during Wilson's time, it created its own miscarriages of justice, most notably the imprisonment of most of the country's Japanese-Americans, including thousands of citizens, following the outset of American involvement in the war in 1941. Few German-Americans faced detention or slander during World War II, in large part because they had by then blended in with the American population at large.

Nations united. In 1945, as World War II drew to a close, world leaders established the United Nations (right, international headquarters, New York City). The U.N. replaced the League of Nations with a structure that protected the authority of world powers.

Participation in the United Nations after World War II by the U.S. and other leading nations helped achieve many of the very goals Wilson had envisioned during his Presidency. Wilson's practice of using diplomacy as a way to avoid warfare and his commitment to the influence many nations can have on one country are now an accepted part of international relations. Such beliefs have earned the term "Wilsonian" in his honor.

A less visible legacy of Wilson's Presidency became the changing nature of the United States itself. No longer was it a collection of immigrant groups loosely tied together in the nation's towns and regions. The residents began to think of themselves as Americans first, immigrants second (if at all). The notion developed of what it meant to be American. Even immigrants wanted to become Americanized—to speak English, to adopt the habits and customs of native-born Americans, to be viewed as equals. Greater tolerance began to emerge of the differences in others that remained, too. Such changes made it easier for the nation to fight wars, honor the intentions of the U.S. Constitution, and contribute to the forward momentum of the country. The birth of national unity, however painful it was at the time, may be one of the most lasting results of all from the First World War.

Wilson's vision on the eve of America's declaration of war became the reality with time: "We are provincials no longer," he proclaimed during his second inaugural address on March 5, 1917. He explained how events such as the sinking of the *Lusitania* "have made us citizens of the world. There can be no turning back. . . . And yet we are not the less Americans on that account. We shall be the more American if we but remain true to the principles in which we have been bred. . . . the principles of a liberated mankind."

Guide to
WARTIME PRESIDENTS

Wartime presents special challenges to Presidents who must balance the needs for national security against the rights of individual citizens. What follows is an examination of how freedom has fared on the home front during nine of the nation's wars.

THE QUASI-WAR

DATES: **1797–1800**

U.S. PRESIDENT: **John Adams**

ADVERSARY: **France.** Although no war was ever officially declared, a sequence of skirmishes took place in the Atlantic Ocean between pro-U.S. and French ships.

Unraveling freedom on the home front: Concerns that the unrest of the French Revolution could spread through French immigrants into the United States helped fuel Congressional consideration of what became known as the Alien and Sedition Acts of 1798. The Federalist Party of President John Adams pushed through the legislation against the opposition of politicians allied with Vice President Thomas Jefferson, who viewed the legislation as too harsh and politically motivated.

The four acts made it more difficult for foreigners living in America to become U.S. citizens (Naturalization Act), permitted the jailing and deportation of foreign citizens of enemy nations who lived in the U.S. (Alien Enemies Act), allowed suspicious immigrants regardless of their nationality to be jailed and deported (Alien Friends Act), and silenced critical voices in the American news media (Sedition Act).

Historians rank the acts as among the most repressive wartime legislation ever enacted in the United States, and they criticize John Adams for signing them into law. Adams may have been influenced to do so by the strong support his wife Abigail gave to the legislation, having been offended by the harsh and often false accusations then being made about her husband in the partisan press. Although the Alien Acts saw little use, prosecutions under the Sedition Act led to the conviction of about a dozen journalists, all of whom were advocates for the opposition party. Federalists hoped to retain control of the Presidency during the next election by silencing these voices. Instead their repressive tactics bolstered Jefferson's party and resulted in his election as President in 1800. No Federalist ever won another presidential election. By 1802 the Alien and Sedition Acts had either expired or been repealed.

John Adams severely curtailed freedoms on the home front during his Presidency.

Quote: *"I wish the laws of our country were competent to punish the stirrer up of sedition. . . . And in times like the present, a more careful and attentive watch ought to be kept over foreigners."* —Abigail Adams, May 26, 1798

WAR OF 1812

DATES: **1812–1815**

U.S. PRESIDENT: **James Madison**

ADVERSARY: **Great Britain**

Unraveling freedom on the home front: President James Madison, an ardent critic of the wartime measures enacted during the Presidency of John Adams, insisted that his government would tolerate criticism during the War of 1812. Thus no wartime measures were adopted to suppress dissent even though there was widespread disagreement about the need for the war. Many members of Congress had voted against the declaration of war, with the northeastern United States being most notably opposed to fighting the British. The War of 1812 represents the rare instance in U.S. history when conflicts abroad did not foster the unraveling of freedom at home.

The right of free speech must be honored during wartime, asserted James Madison, as a sign of the nation's commitment to freedom.

Quote: *"Some degree of abuse is inseparable from the proper use of everything; and in no instance is this more true than in that of the press. . . . It is better to leave a few of its noxious branches to their luxuriant growth, than, by pruning them away, to injure the vigor of those yielding the proper fruits. . . . To the press alone, chequered as it is with abuses, the world is indebted for all the triumphs which have been gained by reason and humanity over error and oppression."* —James Madison, 1800

CIVIL WAR

DATES: **1861–1865**

U.S. PRESIDENT: **Abraham Lincoln**

ADVERSARY: **Confederate States of America (former southern United States)**

Unraveling freedom on the home front: When the fighting of the Civil War began, President Abraham Lincoln imposed emergency restrictions in the face of unfolding rebellion. He ordered that suspected rebels be arrested and jailed, denying them their usual *habeas corpus* right to a trial until their trustworthiness could be determined. He permitted members of the military to arrest and try civilians who protested the war, too. These measures were principally used in the early days of the war as leaders assessed who would stand behind the Union and who would join the Confederacy.

Lincoln asserted that, as President, he had the authority to take these extraordinary steps in order to secure the nation's defense in the face of rebellion. He maintained that the nation could not afford to wait for Congress to consider whether or not to pass laws in favor of his wartime restrictions. Lincoln's extraordinary use of authority caused some concern, but the short-term nature of his actions kept criticism from growing. Historians have generally viewed his actions as warranted within the context of the time. Congress later affirmed the steps he had taken by passing laws that matched his executive orders.

Technological advances, such as the telegraph, photography, and high-speed printing presses, made it possible for the news media to keep the public informed about the war with timely news coverage. Lincoln did not attempt to silence his critics, either in the media or in Congress. However, military commanders did at times arrest and try civilians who criticized the government's war effort; Lincoln discouraged such steps but did not work as hard as he could have to prevent them from occurring.

Quote: *"I may not have made as great a President as some other men, but I believe I have kept these discordant elements together as well as anyone could." —Abraham Lincoln during the Civil War*

Initially Abraham Lincoln (right, visiting the battlefront) restricted individual rights when civil war developed in the U.S., but his limitations were short-lived.

WORLD WAR I

DATES: **1914–1918**

U.S. INVOLVEMENT: **1917–1918**

U.S. PRESIDENT: **Woodrow Wilson**

ADVERSARIES: **Germany, Austria-Hungary, Bulgaria, the Ottoman Empire**

Unraveling freedom on the home front: President Woodrow Wilson's 1917 call to make the world safe for democracy led to an erosion of democratic freedoms at home with the passage of such wartime legislation as the Espionage Act of 1917, the Sedition Act of 1918, and the Alien Act of 1918. Wilson and other members of his administration asserted that the laws were needed to secure the home front from spies and the influence of critics. The repressive use of these

Woodrow Wilson spoke about the virtues of freedom and democracy even as his government curtailed civil liberties.

laws continued during the Red Scare that followed the war. Such actions tested the First Amendment right of free speech, and court cases arising from the era led to a clearer and more broadly defined understanding of this right.

An extensive government-led propaganda effort created a surge in patriotism and left immigrants and other outsiders vulnerable to charges of being un-American. German-Americans and political radicals faced increased scrutiny, suspicion, and pressure to shed their cultural connections to their mother countries or their nontraditional beliefs. Citizens acting in the name of patriotism punished those who seemed out of step with the war effort in a wave of vigilante violence. This wartime atmosphere created a sense of Americanism that led many outsiders to shed their immigrant traditions in an effort to be viewed as more American.

Quote: *"I am in a hurry to have an opportunity to have a line-up and let the men who are thinking first of other countries stand on one side . . . and all those that are for America first, last, and all the time, on the other side. . . . We constantly discipline our fellow-citizens by having an opinion about them. That is the sort of discipline we ought now to administer to everybody who is not to the very core of his heart an American. Just have an opinion about him and let him experience the atmospheric effects of that opinion." —Woodrow Wilson, October, 11, 1915, speaking at the 25th anniversary celebration of the Daughters of the American Revolution*

Franklin D. Roosevelt (center), who forged wartime alliances with Soviet leader Joseph Stalin (left) and Great Britain's Winston Churchill (right), avoided repeating most of the home-front mistakes from the First World War even as he committed new ones.

WORLD WAR II

DATES: **1939–1945**

U.S. INVOLVEMENT: **1941–1945**

U.S. PRESIDENTS: **Franklin D. Roosevelt, Harry S. Truman**

ADVERSARIES: **Germany, Italy, Japan, and six other Axis powers**

Unraveling freedom on the home front: Although the United States avoided repeating many of the practices that had restricted civil liberties during World War I—propaganda efforts were typically more restrained, for example, and German-Americans generally avoided the suspicions that had haunted them in the earlier world war—new infringements on home-front freedom developed with the new war. Most notable was the wholesale incarceration of most of the nation's Japanese-American population following the bombing of Pearl Harbor on December 7, 1941. At first only a limited number of enemy aliens were arrested and jailed, but eventually some 120,000 first- and second-generation Japanese-Americans, including thousands of American citizens, were rounded up and secured indefinitely in concentration-camp-style compounds. Many remained imprisoned for the duration of the war.

Other measures that challenged the freedom of U.S. residents included the creation in 1938 of the House Un-American Activities Committee (HUAC), a group that accused a broad range of individuals and groups of working against the principles of the nation. Even organizations such as the Boy Scouts and Camp Fire Girls faced charges of supporting communism, the political beliefs practiced by the Soviet Union, a one-time ally of Germany. The Federal Bureau of Investigation pursued similar inquiries under the leadership of J. Edgar Hoover. Such efforts laid the groundwork for further erosions of civil liberties during the Cold War that developed after World War II.

Quote: *"A democracy fighting a total war will fight it more enthusiastically and effectively if it knows what is going on, and if it feels that its leaders trust it with as much information as it can possibly be given without giving aid and comfort to the enemy." —Elmer Davis, director of the Office of War Information, the nation's propaganda office during World War II*

THE COLD WAR

DATES: **circa 1945–1992**

U.S. PRESIDENTS: **Harry S. Truman, Dwight D. Eisenhower, John F. Kennedy, Lyndon B. Johnson, Richard Nixon, Gerald R. Ford, Jimmy Carter, Ronald Reagan, George H.W. Bush**

ADVERSARIES: **The Soviet Union, other countries governed by communism**

Unraveling freedom on the home front: At no time during the decades-long Cold War were home-front freedoms more challenged than during the so-called McCarthy era of the 1940s and 1950s. At that time politicians capitalized on the fears of communist influence in order to gain notoriety and power by leveling charges of anti-Americanism and pro-communism at thousands of respected, loyal citizens. The period is named after its most vocal and persistent spokesperson, Republican Senator Joseph R. McCarthy of Wisconsin, who directed his accusations from his post as chairman of a subcommittee tasked with managing Senate investigations. Congressional representatives pursued similar tactics through a companion body, the House Un-American Activities Committee (HUAC).

Among those falsely accused of being communist sympathizers were noted actors, artists, writers, politicians, and intellectuals, even figures as well-regarded as General George C. Marshall of World War II fame. Only after years of abuse did political leaders and members of the media muster the momentum to systematically expose the false nature of the accusations being leveled and close down the misplaced investigations of HUAC and McCarthy's subcommittee.

Quote: *"Scaremongers and the hate mongers. . . . have created such a wave of fear and uncertainty that their attacks upon our liberties go almost unchallenged. Many people are growing frightened—and frightened people don't protest....When even one American—who has done nothing wrong—is forced by fear to shut his mind and close his mouth, then all Americans are in peril."* –Harry S. Truman, in a nationally broadcast speech to members of the American Legion, August 14, 1951

In 1987 Ronald Reagan spoke near the Cold War barrier that divided the city of Berlin and challenged authorities to "tear down this wall."

VIETNAM WAR

DATES: **1957–1975**

U.S. PRESIDENTS: **Dwight D. Eisenhower, John F. Kennedy, Lyndon B. Johnson, Richard Nixon**

ADVERSARY: **North Vietnam**

Unraveling freedom on the home front: As the war in Vietnam escalated in length and scale, Americans became divided in their support over what was portrayed as an essential anti-communist fight of the Cold War. During the administrations of Lyndon B. Johnson and Richard Nixon, young people facing the threat of being drafted into military service began to protest against the war. Conflicts developed between protesters who doubted the war's importance and war supporters who viewed the anti-war demonstrations as acts of anti-Americanism. President Nixon ordered secret investigations of thousands of citizens suspected of disloyalty, and efforts were made to disrupt the effectiveness of the peace groups by planting spies and troublemakers within their organizations.

Mistrust developed between the Nixon administration and the news media, too, particularly after reporters began to question the soundness of the U.S. military strategy and the accuracy of official reports about the conflict. Tensions flared in 1971 after the *New York Times* began publishing analyses and excerpts from what became known as the "Pentagon Papers." The government tried to suppress the publication of the federal documents, which had been leaked to the *Times* by a former government analyst, claiming that their publication would endanger national security. When editors at the *Times* halted their publication, the *Washington Post* picked up the material. Within days the U.S. Supreme Court was evaluating this argument over free speech versus national security. The Court ruled in favor of the newspapers. Such disputes between citizens and government officials undermined national confidence in the war.

Quote: *"To you, the great silent majority of my fellow Americans, I ask for your support. . . . The more divided we are at home, the less likely the enemy is to negotiate. . . . North Vietnam cannot defeat or humiliate the United States. Only Americans can do that." —Richard M. Nixon, nationally televised address, November 3, 1969*

Home-front tensions over the Vietnam War prompted Lyndon B. Johnson (below, preparing a wartime speech) to cancel his reelection bid.

AFGHANISTAN and IRAQ WARS

DATES: **2003–present**

U.S. PRESIDENTS: **George W. Bush, Barack Obama**

ADVERSARIES: **The standing governments of Afghanistan and Iraq as well as insurgent forces in those regions**

George W. Bush (above, touring a military site) asserted that threats of terrorism justified the limiting of home-front civil liberties.

Unraveling freedom on the home front: The Afghanistan and Iraq Wars developed after the 9-11 terrorist attacks of 2001, a breach of national security that led initially to the invasion of Afghanistan and, eventually and more controversially, Iraq. Congress passed sweeping legislation soon after 9-11 that expanded the government's ability to spy on its citizens and other residents in an effort to identify terrorists. The Patriot Act gave investigators access to everything from an individual's phone call records to lists of books checked out by library patrons. As with the Espionage Act of 1917, many of the provisions had been crafted prior to national security threats. Whereas before the 9-11 attack they might have been dismissed as infringements of individual rights, now they gained acceptance as essential tools for homeland security.

During the administration of George W. Bush, suspected terrorists were classified as "enemy combatants," a determination that denied them the rights normally awarded to prisoners of war. The U.S. government came under increasing criticism as details surfaced of secret apprehensions and out-sourced torturing of suspected enemies. Long-term detention of suspected terrorists at an off-shore military prison located at Guantanamo Bay, Cuba, created judicial debates at home over the legality of holding such prisoners without trial.

After taking office in 2009, President Barack Obama found it difficult to make a clean break from past practices, although he did firmly reject the use of torture. His early efforts to close the Guantanamo Bay prison were unsuccessful, however, and the rights of enemy combatants remained a subject of debate even as combat escalated in Afghanistan.

Quote: *"Americans are a free people, who know that freedom is the right of every person and the future of every nation. The liberty we prize is not America's gift to the world, it is God's gift to humanity." —George W. Bush, State of the Union Address, January 28, 2003*

TIMELINE

Entries in this timeline track major events in the following categories:

W The life of Woodrow Wilson

L The history of the *Lusitania*

★ The history of U.S. involvement in World War I and related key dates

G General events, including developments on the U.S. home front during World War I

1856

W Woodrow Wilson is born in Staunton, Virginia, on December 29.

1890

W Woodrow Wilson joins the faculty of Princeton University in Princeton, New Jersey.

1902

W In June Woodrow Wilson becomes president of Princeton University.

1907

L In September the *Lusitania* embarks from Liverpool, England, on her maiden voyage, bound for New York City.

1910

W Woodrow Wilson is elected governor of New Jersey in November. He assumes office on January 17, 1911.

1911

W Woodrow Wilson meets Edward M. House in November as he prepares to run for President of the United States; House becomes one of Wilson's political advisors.

1912

G The *Titanic* sinks on April 15 during its maiden voyage across the Atlantic.

W Woodrow Wilson wins the presidential election on November 5. He is sworn in as the nation's 28th Chief Executive on March 4, 1913.

1914

★ The assassination on June 28 of Archduke Francis Ferdinand of Austria-Hungary sets off the chain of events that leads to the First World War.

★ Germany invades Belgium on August 4, drawing England and France into the conflict.

W Woodrow Wilson's wife Ellen dies on August 6.

1915

G More than 1,000 women from around the world, including prominent social activist Jane Addams, hold a conference in the Netherlands to advocate for a peaceful solution to the First World War; they establish the Women's International League for Peace and Freedom to support this goal, with Addams serving as the group's first president.

L On April 30 *U-boat 20* departs the naval base at Emden, Germany, under the command of Walther Schwieger with a mission to patrol the shipping lanes for the enemy port of Liverpool, England.

L The *Lusitania* sets sail on May 1 from New York City under the command of William Turner bound for its home port of Liverpool, England.

L A torpedo fired from German *U-boat 20* causes the British ocean liner *Lusitania* to sink off the coast of Ireland on May 7. Among the dead are 128 Americans.

L On May 13 *U-boat 20* returns to Germany after traveling over 3,000 nautical miles. The crew is greeted with three cheers from fellow sailors.

W Woodrow Wilson and Edith Bolling Galt announce their engagement on October 6. They marry on December 18.

1916

W On November 7 Woodrow Wilson wins election to a second term as President of the United States, running with the campaign slogan, "He kept us out of war."

L Captain Walther Schwieger blows up *U-boat 20* after the submarine runs aground along the coast of Denmark.

1917

★ Woodrow Wilson addresses a joint session of Congress on April 2 and requests that war be declared on Germany. The declaration is made on April 6.

★ Woodrow Wilson creates the Committee on Public Information (CPI) and appoints George Creel as its director.

★ In June Congress passes the Espionage Act of 1917, a wartime measure intent on assuring the nation's security during the First World War.

G Later that month Sheriff Harry Wheeler deputizes thousands of volunteers to help expel 1,200 striking mine workers and their family members from the area around Bisbee, Arizona.

L Captain Walther Schwieger and his crew are lost at sea aboard German *U-boat 88*.

G Victor Berger, a German-American, loses the right to mail his Socialist newspaper, the *Milwaukee Leader,* after being charged with violating the Espionage Act of 1917. Further charges arise in 1918 after he continues to publish critical comments about the U.S. war effort.

G The U.S. House and Senate adopt the 18th Amendment, legislation that prohibits the production and consumption of alcoholic beverages in the country. It is ratified in January of 1919 and takes effect a year later.

1918

★ In January Woodrow Wilson presents what become known as his Fourteen Points for world peace. These ideas form the basis of his negotiating strategy during the 1919 peace conference for ending the First World War.

G Robert Prager, an immigrant coal miner in Illinois, is murdered by a vigilante mob on April 5 because of suspicions that he may be a spy.

★ In May Congress amends the Espionage Act of 1917 by adding a series of restrictions known as the Sedition Act of 1918.

G Eugene Debs condemns the jailing of anti-war protesters during a speech in Canton, Ohio, on June 16. Two weeks later he is arrested and charged with violating the Espionage Act of 1917. Debs is convicted on three counts during a September trial and sentenced to ten years in prison. He remains out of jail as he appeals his case to the U.S. Supreme Court.

★ Congress passes the Alien Act of 1918, making it easier to deport aliens who appear threatening because of their radical or non-traditional beliefs.

G During November's mid-term elections, Republicans defeat enough Democrats to gain control of both houses of Congress.

G Victor Berger, a Socialist from Milwaukee, Wisconsin, wins election to the U.S. House of Representatives despite pending charges of having violated the Espionage Act of 1917.

★ Kaiser Wilhelm II flees Germany on November 9, giving up his rights to rule the country.

★ The fighting of World War I stops at 11 a.m. on November 11 with the signing of an armistice, or cease-fire agreement, by German officials.

★ Woodrow Wilson departs the United States on December 4 bound for Europe and a peace conference in Paris.

1919

★ On January 12 Woodrow Wilson and other delegates from the victorious nations begin meeting in Paris to determine the terms for a peace treaty with Germany and other wartime enemies.

G Victor Berger is sentenced to 20 years in prison for publishing articles in the *Milwaukee Leader* that were critical of the government's war effort. He remains out of jail as he appeals his case to the U.S. Supreme Court.

G After losing his Supreme Court appeal of the charges that he violated the Espionage Act of 1917, Eugene Debs begins serving his 10-year prison sentence in April.

G The U.S. House and Senate approve adoption of the 19th Amendment, granting women the right to vote. The amendment earns its final ratification vote on August 18, 1920, and takes effect in time for the 1920 fall elections.

★ Representatives sign the Treaty of Versailles on June 28, signaling the end of World War I. Wilson departs Europe and returns to the United States on July 8, intent on securing ratification of the treaty by the U.S. Senate, as required by the nation's Constitution.

★ Woodrow Wilson abolishes the Committee on Public Information (CPI) by executive order on August 21.

★ On September 2 Woodrow Wilson embarks on a cross-country speaking tour to urge ratification of the Treaty of Versailles. He collapses hours after speaking in Colorado on September 25 and is rushed back to the White House.

W Woodrow Wilson's health deteriorates significantly after he has a stroke on October 2.

L Captain William Turner retires in November from service on the Cunard line of cruise ships. He is 63 years old.

G Members of the U.S. House of Representatives refuse to let Victor Berger assume the seat he won during the 1918 election. After Wisconsin voters re-elect him to the vacant seat, he is still denied entry to the House by a vote taken on January 10, 1920.

★ The U.S. Senate fails to approve the Treaty of Versailles, falling far short of the required two-thirds' majority, with 53 Senators voting against passage and 38 supporting it.

1920

★ On March 19 the U.S. Senate fails on a second attempt to approve the Treaty of Versailles. Supporters fall seven votes short in their effort.

★ Congress repeals the Sedition Act of 1918. The Espionage Act of 1917 remains in force.

W Woodrow Wilson is awarded the 1919 Nobel Peace Prize.

1921

G The U.S. Supreme Court overturns the conviction of Victor Berger as having violated the Espionage Act of 1917, asserting that he had not received fair treatment by his judge.

W Woodrow Wilson's Presidency ends on March 4 with the inauguration of Warren G. Harding as the nation's 29th President.

★ The U.S. Senate approves separate peace treaties with Germany and other hostile nations, officially concluding the First World War.

G Warren G. Harding pardons Eugene Debs on Christmas Day, ending more than two years of imprisonment.

1922

G Victor Berger wins election to the House of Representatives and is seated without objection. He is reelected in 1924 and 1926.

1923

G President Warren G. Harding dies during a cross-country train trip on August 2; Vice President Calvin Coolidge steps in as the nation's 30th Chief Executive.

1924

W Woodrow Wilson dies on February 3 in Washington, D.C., at the age of 67.

1926

G Eugene Debs dies on October 20 near Chicago, Illinois, at age 70.

1929

G Victor Berger dies on August 7 in Milwaukee, Wisconsin, following a traffic accident, at age 69.

1931

G Jane Addams becomes the first woman from the United States to be awarded the Nobel Peace Prize.

1933

L Captain William Turner dies on June 23 near Liverpool, England, at the age of 76.

G Congress and the states vote to repeal the 18th Amendment, overturning the prohibition of the consumption of alcoholic beverages that began in 1920.

1935

G Jane Addams dies on May 21 in Chicago, Illinois, at the age of 74.

L Divers visit the wreck of the *Lusitania* for the first time.

1938

G Edward M. House dies on March 28 in New York City at age 79.

1939

G World War II breaks out in Europe with Germany's invasion of Poland on September 1.

1941

G The United States joins World War II by declaring war on Japan following the Japanese bombing of U.S. naval ships anchored at Pearl Harbor, Hawaii, on December 7. Germany declares war on the U.S. four days later.

1945

G World War II concludes with the surrenders of Germany on May 7 and Japan on August 14.

G On June 26, delegates from 50 nations at a conference held in San Francisco, California, agree to establish an international organization devoted to world peace. This group, called the United Nations, secures an internationally-approved charter on October 24 and holds its first meeting in London during 1946.

1961

W Edith Wilson, widow of President Woodrow Wilson, dies on December 28 in Washington, D.C., at age 89.

1993

L Scientist and explorer Robert Ballard surveys the wreck of the *Lusitania* and corroborates the theory that secondary explosions aboard the sinking ship were the result of the ignition of coal dust within the ship's coal bunkers.

NOTES AND ACKNOWLEDGMENTS

RESOURCE NOTES: Researching a nonfiction book requires the mindset of a detective and the patience of someone fishing. You do your best to search in productive waters, and then you wait to land just the right catch of relevant facts. The research for some books takes you on the road; this one took me to the library. Instead of visiting locations to set a scene, I needed to go back in time to find an earlier era. Books took me there.

Unfortunately, my topic has rarely been the focus of scholarly study, so I had to wade through sources that nibbled around the edges of my search. One find led to the next as I undertook a sequential detective hunt for the full picture of the home-front dynamics during World War I. Often a passing reference in a newer book would lead to more details buried in an older book that had been written during an era when more scholars studied the First World War.

The deeper I dug, the more struck I was by parallels that exist between the First World War and our 21st-century wars in Iraq and Afghanistan. Acts of terrorism—the sinking of the *Lusitania* in 1915 and the 9-11 airline hijackings and crashes of 2001—fueled political and popular calls for combat. Presidents with deep religious convictions framed their war plans within the context of a fight for democracy. Patriotism ran high in each era, and the charge of being unpatriotic easily undercut (and all but silenced) dissenting voices. Wartime advocates converted symbols of opponents (for example sauerkraut or French fries) into icons of the cause (such as liberty cabbage and freedom fries). People, including American citizens, who looked or sounded like the enemy all too often became the enemy, whether or not such profiling was justified.

While I worked, these parallels jumped out of the records from the past as the latest example of how history does, indeed, repeat itself all too easily and often. Perhaps the monumental events that filled the rest of the 20th century overshadowed the lessons the nation might have learned after World War I. I hope that by calling them back into memory, the next generation will bring richer understanding should similar challenges present themselves in the future.

Frequently I'm asked, where do you get the ideas for your books? Rarely is the answer as clear in my mind as it is for *Unraveling Freedom*. A 2006 article in the *New York Times* placed the first clue at my feet with the intriguing headline: "Silence Broken, Pardons Granted 88 Years After Crimes of Sedition." The story detailed the history of Montana's campaign against German-Americans during World War I, and it stunned me with accounts of persecution and injustice that I had not imagined possible in this country. Thus began my effort to write this book. Although my research eventually took me in a different direction, I'm grateful to have been introduced through this newspaper story to the research conducted by Clemens P. Work and his students at the University of Montana School of Journalism.

The accompanying bibliography records the full range of sources consulted during my research journey, including Professor Work's book *Darkest Before Dawn*. Several sources deserve particular acknowledgment. I am indebted to Diana Preston for recording so many personal stories and details in her book Lusitania: *An Epic Tragedy*. Her in-depth research of this topic provided a foundation for the first chapter of my book. Fresh biographies of Woodrow Wilson by such historians as John A. Thompson and H.W. Brands helped me convey events of the era and the mindset of our nation's 28th President in the chapters that followed. Two historians came closest to examining my topic in their own research: Geoffrey R. Stone, author of *Perilous Times,* and Christopher Capozzola with his book *Uncle Sam Wants You.* Works cited by these historians led to my discovery of earlier relevant works, including Joan M. Jensen's *The Price of Vigilance* and Robert H. Ferrell's study, *Woodrow Wilson and World War I.*

Unraveling Freedom is the fourth book I have written about the early 20th century and the Presidency of Woodrow Wilson. Thus I returned to some old friends in the course of my research, too, including Robert M. Crunden's *Ministers of Reform* and the book *Voices of a Nation* by Jean Folkerts and Dwight L. Teeter, Jr. A collection of essays edited by David P. Bensler and Walter F. W. Lohnes on *Teaching German in America* added topic-specific information to my search, as well.

Working on this book reminds me more than ever that the study of history relies on the layering of generations of research, each scholar reviewing the insights of the past, identifying additional material for study, and using new lenses to examine old evidence, all for the cause of adding one more book or article to a foundation of understanding that stretches back into the dusty reaches of the past. It is my great privilege and good fortune to work with the output of these lifetime scholars and then shyly, respectfully, to offer up a new accounting of the past. I could not do my own work without these career historians. Thank you.

ACKNOWLEDGMENTS: I am honored by and grateful to historian Christopher Capozzola for reviewing this book in proof form. I owe much gratitude to the Council for Wisconsin Writers and Edenfred, a cultural retreat center in Madison, Wisconsin, for sponsoring a week-long residency for me at this magical setting during the summer of 2009. Many thanks to David Wells, Jan Terry, and Tom Terry for making my stay at Edenfred so productive. I wrote my first draft of Chapter 1 during this residency. My efforts were aided by the beautiful and haunting background music that was provided throughout my stay by fellow residents Darryl Harper, jazz clarinetist, and Kevin Harris, jazz pianist. Their soulful compositions grounded me in a peaceful place that gave me the strength to return day after day to the awful realities of the sinking of the *Lusitania.* Thank you, Kevin and Darryl.

Once again I owe appreciation to my Critique Group—Georgia Beaverson, Pam Peres, Judy Bryan, Elizabeth Fixmer, Kathleen Petrella, and Jamie Swenson—for supporting me during this project with your review of early drafts and through your friendship. Thanks go to the full team at National Geographic, too. It's been a particular joy to collaborate for the fourth time in a row with the gifted book designer Marty Ittner and to work again with such favorite NGS staff members as Jennifer Emmett, Nancy Laties Feresten, Lori Epstein, and Jeff Reynolds, and to work for the first time with Jim Hiscott. Thanks, as always, to my local librarians, too.

As for the family and friends who have lived with me through the recent years of life and another book, thank you from my whole heart: my sons Sam and Jake, my parents Dolores and Henry, my brother David, his wife Mary, the caregivers who help me become limber again after all the sitting that goes into a book, and friends near and far—from Hester and Peggy in town to residents of the Emerson Hotel now scattered nationwide to roving friends like John and Ann. As for Kedron, home-front wise, and the true-blue friend to whom this book is dedicated, I simply say, "Thank you."

BIBLIOGRAPHY

Adams, Abigail. *New Letters of Abigail Adams, 1788-1801.* New York, New York: Houghton Mifflin Company, 1947.

"All Disloyal Men Warned by Gregory." *New York Times,* November 21, 1917.

American Mining Congress, Arizona Chapter. "Deportations from Bisbee: and a Resume of Other Troubles in Arizona." Published circa 1917. Available online at: http://www.library.arizona.edu/exhibits/bisbee/docs/deport.html.

Ballard, Robert D. *Robert Ballard's Lusitania.* Toronto, Ontario: Madison Press Books, 2007.

Beck, James M. "President Voices Nobler Sentiment of U.S." *New York Times,* April 8, 1917.

Bollinger, Lee C. and Geoffrey R. Stone, editors. *Eternally Vigilant: Free Speech in the Modern Era.* Chicago, Illinois: The University of Chicago Press, 2002.

Boyd, Gerald M. "Raze Berlin Wall, Reagan Urges Soviet." *New York Times,* June 13, 1987.

Brands, H. W. *Woodrow Wilson.* The American Presidents. Arthur M. Schlesinger, Jr., gen. ed. New York, New York: Times Books, Henry Holt and Company, 2003.

Bubser, Reinhold K. "Speaking and Teaching German in Iowa During World War I: A Historical Perspective." In *Teaching German in America: Prolegomena to a History,* edited by David P. Benseler, Walter F. W. Lohnes, 206-14. Madison, Wisconsin: The University of Wisconsin Press, 1988.

Capozzola, Christopher. *Uncle Sam Wants You: World War I and the Making of the Modern American Citizen.* New York, New York: Oxford University Press, 2008.

"Capt. Eddie Rickenbacker Is Dead at 82." *New York Times,* July 24, 1973.

"Congress Cheers as Wilson Urges Curb on Plotters." *New York Times,* December 8, 1915, pp. 1, 7.

Crunden, Robert M. *Ministers of Reform: The Progressives' Achievement in American Civilization, 1889-1920.* Urbana, Illinois: University of Illinois Press, 1984.

Daniels, Roger. *Coming to America: A History of Immigration and Ethnicity in American Life.* New York, New York: HarperCollins Publishers, 2002.

____. *Not Like Us: Immigrants and Minorities in America, 1890-1924.* Chicago, Illinois: Ivan. R. Dee, 1997.

"Debs Arrested; Sedition Charged." *New York Times,* July 1, 1918, pp. 1, 6.

"Debs Case in High Court." *New York Times,* January 28, 1919.

Debs, Eugene V. *Writings and Speeches of Eugene V. Debs.* New York, New York: Hermitage Press, 1948.

Elliot, Jonathan, editor. *The Debates in the Several State Conventions on the Adoption of the Federal Constitution.* Second edition. Vol. IV. Washington, D.C.: Jonathan Elliot, 1836.

"E. V. Debs Declines to Offer Defense." *New York Times,* September 12, 1918.

Ferrell, Robert H. *Woodrow Wilson and World War I.* New York, New York: Harper & Row, 1985.

"Find Debs Guilty of Disloyal Acts." *New York Times,* September 13, 1918, pp. 1, 4.

Folkerts, Jean and Dwight L. Teeter, Jr. *Voices of a Nation: A History of Mass Media in the United States.* Boston, Massachusetts: Allyn & Bacon, 2002.

Frank, Ted E. "The Dawn of Teaching German in the Public Schools: A Study of DER AMERIKANISCHE LESER, Cincinnati, 1854." In *Teaching German in America: Prolegomena to a History,* edited by David P. Benseler, Walter F. W. Lohnes, 120-32. Madison, Wisconsin: The University of Wisconsin Press, 1988.

"The Great Wobbly Drive." *The Bisbee Daily Review* (Bisbee, Arizona), July 13, 1917.

Hawley, Ellis W. *The Great War and the Search for a Modern Order: A History of the American People and Their Institutions, 1917-1933.* New York, New York: St. Martin's Press, 1979.

Herndon, William H. and Jesse W. Weik. *Herndon's Lincoln.* Urbana, Illinois: University of Illinois Press, 2006.

Hirschfeld, Charles. "The Transformation of American Life." In *World War I: A Turning Point in Modern History,* edited by Jack J. Roth, 63-81. New York, New York: Alfred A. Knopf, 1967.

Hohlfeld, Alexander R. and Cora Lee Nollendorfs. "Address by Professor Alexander R. Hohlfeld, University of Wisconsin, to the Graduating Class of the National Teachers Seminary at Milwaukee on Thursday, 20 June 1918." In *Teaching German in America: Prolegomena to a History,* edited by David P. Benseler, Walter F. W. Lohnes, 197-205. Madison, Wisconsin: The University of Wisconsin Press, 1988.

"House Defeats Censorship Law by 184-144." *New York Times,* June 1, 1917, pp. 1, 2.

"Is Hatred of the German in the Present Crisis a Duty?" *Current Opinion,* Vol. LXV, July-December, 1918, edited by Edward J. Wheeler, 383-84. New York, New York: The Current Literature Publishing Company, 1918.

Jensen, Joan M. *The Price of Vigilance.* Chicago, Illinois: Rand McNally and Company, 1968.

Kennedy, David M. *Over Here: The First World War and American Society.* New York, New York: Oxford University Press, 1980.

Lepore, Jill. "Preexisting condition." *The New Yorker,* December 7, 2009, pp. 29-30.

Maynard, W. Barksdale. *Woodrow Wilson: Princeton to the Presidency.* New Haven, Connecticut: Yale University Press, 2008.

McGerr, Michael. *A Fierce Discontent: The Rise and Fall of the Progressive Movement in America.* New York, New York: Oxford University Press, 2005.

Murphy, Paul L. *World War I and the Origin of Civil Liberties in the United States.* New York, New York: W.W. Norton & Company, 1979.

Murray, Robert K. *Red Scare: A Study of National Hysteria, 1919-1920.* New York, New York: McGraw-Hill Book Company, 1955.

Nollendorfs, Cora Lee. "The First World War and the Survival of German Studies: With a Tribute to Alexander R. Hohlfeld." In *Teaching German in America: Prolegomena to a History,* edited by David P. Benseler, Walter F. W. Lohnes, 176-96. Madison, Wisconsin: The University of Wisconsin Press, 1988.

Preston, Diana. *Lusitania: An Epic Tragedy.* New York, New York: Berkley Books, 2003.

RESOURCE GUIDE

Public Papers of the Presidents, Harry S. Truman [online]. Harry S. Truman Library and Museum. "Address at the Dedication of the New Washington Headquarters of the American Legion, August 14, 1951." Available online at: http://www.trumanlibrary.org/publicpapers/index.php?pid=406&st=&st1=.

Schmidt, Henry J. "The Rhetoric of Survival: The Germanist in America, 1900-1925." In *Teaching German in America: Prolegomena to a History,* edited by David P. Benseler, Walter F. W. Lohnes, 165-75. Madison, Wisconsin: The University of Wisconsin Press, 1988.

Stone, Geoffrey R. *Perilous Times: Free Speech in Wartime.* New York, New York: W. W. Norton & Company, 2004.

"Swears Debs Upheld Anti-War Program." *New York Times,* September 11, 1918.

Thompson, John A. *Woodrow Wilson.* London, England: Pearson Education Limited, 2002.

"Wilson Calls for American Line-Up." *New York Times,* October 12, 1915.

"Wilson Demands Press Censorship." *New York Times,* May 23, 1917.

Woolley, John T. and Gerhardt Peters, editors. The American Presidency Project [online]. Santa Barbara, CA. "Woodrow Wilson: Address to a Joint Session of Congress Requesting a Declaration of War Against Germany, April 2, 1917." Available online at: http://www.presidency.ucsb.edu/ws/index.php?pid=65366&st=&st1=

_____ . The American Presidency Project [online]. Santa Barbara, CA. "Richard Nixon: Address to the Nation on the War in Vietnam, November 3, 1969." Available online at: http://www.presidency.ucsb.edu/ws/?pid=2303.

_____. The American Presidency Project [online]. Santa Barbara, CA. "George W. Bush: Address before a Joint Session of the Congress on the State of the Union, January 28, 2003." Available online at: http://www.presidency.ucsb.edu/ws/?pid=29645.

Work, Clemens P. *Darkest Before Dawn: Sedition and Free Speech in the American West.* Albuquerque, New Mexico: University of New Mexico Press, 2005.

Zeydel, Edwin H. "The Teaching of German in the United States from Colonial Times Through World War I." In *Teaching German in America: Prolegomena to a History,* edited by David P. Benseler, Walter F. W. Lohnes, 15-54. Madison, Wisconsin: The University of Wisconsin Press, 1988.

Books of General Interest

Bausum, Ann. *Denied, Detained, Deported: Stories from the Dark Side of American Immigration.* Washington, D.C.: National Geographic Society, 2009.

A source for more information about the Red Scare of 1919 (see chapter 5).

_____. *With Courage and Cloth: Winning the Fight for a Woman's Right to Vote.* Washington, D.C.: National Geographic Society, 2004.

A source for more information about conflicts resulting from Wilson's lack of interest in women's voting rights during his Presidency.

Preston, Diana. Lusitania: *An Epic Tragedy.* New York, New York: Berkley Books, 2003.

An accessible narrative history about the history of the *Lusitania,* particularly its sinking in 1915.

Documentary Films

"The Great War and the Shaping of the 20th Century"
PBS documentary series
http://www.pbs.org/greatwar/

"Last Voyage of the *Lusitania,*"
National Geographic Society documentary, 1996

Places to Visit in Person and Online

The American Presidency Project
Hosted by the University of California, Santa Barbara
Online archive of Woodrow Wilson's major speeches, proclamations, and executive orders
http://www.presidency.ucsb.edu/woodrow_wilson.php

From the Home Front and the Front Lines
Library of Congress (online exhibit)
http://www.loc.gov/exhibits/treasures/homefront-home.html

The Montana Sedition Project
http://www.seditionproject.net/

Online Archive and Photo Essay about *The Stars and Stripes* Military Newspaper
American Memory, Library of Congress
http://memory.loc.gov/ammem/sgphtml/sashtml/sashome.html

Photo Essays and Timeline on World War I
American Memory, Library of Congress
http://memory.loc.gov/ammem/collections/rotogravures/index.html

Woodrow Wilson International Center for Scholars
Washington, D.C.
http://www.wilsoncenter.org/index.cfm?fuseaction=about.woodrow

Woodrow Wilson Papers
Library of Congress webcast
http://www.loc.gov/today/cyberlc/feature_wdesc.php?rec=3303

Woodrow Wilson Presidential Library
Located at his birthplace in Staunton, Virginia
http://www.woodrowwilson.org/learn/learn_show.htm?doc_id=321375

World War I Posters
Library of Congress
http://lcweb2.loc.gov/pp/wwiposhtml/wwiposabt.html

CITATIONS

INTRODUCTION

OPENING QUOTE: p. 8, Woodrow Wilson (WW): "We shall fight…make the world itself at last free." (Woolley and Peters, address by Woodrow Wilson: online resource).

PHOTO CAPTIONS: p. 8, WW: "It would be the irony of fate…with foreign affairs." (Brands: 42).

TEXT: p. 10, WW: "the world must be made safe for democracy." (Woolley and Peters, address by Woodrow Wilson: online resource).

CHAPTER 1—SUNK

OPENING QUOTE: p. 12, Captain Walther Schwieger: "The ship was sinking. . . . too horrible to watch." (Preston: 241).

RAISED QUOTE: p. 19, Margaret Mackworth: "It was freely stated…inspire the world with terror." (Preston: 101).

PHOTO CAPTIONS: p. 13, Oliver Bernard, *Lusitania* survivor: "waving hands and arms…frantic women and children." (Preston: 243); p. 13, *Lusitania* survivor Archie Donald: "was black with people." (Preston: 253); p. 16, Submarine nickname: "assassins of the seas." (Brands: 58); p. 19, *Lusitania* wireless message: "Come at once." (Preston: 201); p. 19, *New York Herald:* "premeditated slaughter." (Ballard: 123); p. 20, Rescuer: "Good gracious, are you alive?" (Preston: 265).

CHAPTER 2—A CALL TO ARMS

OPENING QUOTE: p. 25, Edward House: "We must throw the influence. . . . ever come to a son of man." (Thompson: 118).

RAISED QUOTE: p. 26, WW: "The day has come. . . . she can do no other." (Woolley and Peters, address by Woodrow Wilson: online resource).

TEXT: p. 27, WW speech: "The present submarine warfare. . . . freedom of nations can make them." (Woolley and Peters, address by Woodrow Wilson: on-line resource); p. 28, Robert Lansing: "From the moment…genius as an orator." (Thompson: 150); p. 28, Theodore Roosevelt: "rank… with the great state papers of Washington and Lincoln." (Brands: 85); p. 28, James M. Beck, the *New York Times:* "the sole defect… is its date," and "swiftly followed the crime of the *Lusitania.*" (Beck); p. 29, Edward House: "We shall be at war with Germany within a month." (Preston: 274); p. 31, WW: "We definitely have to be neutral…would wage war on each other." (Thompson: 107); p. 32, WW speech: "We have no quarrel. . . . our national unity of counsel." (Woolley and Peters, address by Woodrow Wilson: online resource).

CHAPTER 3—OFF TO KILL THE HUN

OPENING QUOTE: p. 34, Thomas Gregory: "To all the disloyal. . . . an avenging government." ("All Disloyal Men Warned by Gregory").

RAISED QUOTE: p. 39, William Edgar Borah: "[This act] has all the earmarks. . . . war and patriotism." (Stone: 587).

PHOTO CAPTIONS: p. 37, WW: "had sacrificed their right to civil liberties." (Stone: 137).

TEXT: p. 36, Eugene Debs (ED): "it is extremely dangerous…democracy safe in the world." (Debs: 417); p. 36, ED: "the master class. . . . fought the battles." (Debs: 425); p. 36, ED: "the gentry who are today. . . . whisper their opposition." (Debs: 422); p. 38, Congressman Martin B. Madden: "While we are fighting…autocracy in America." (Stone: 148); p. 38, Congressman Dick Morgan: "In time of great national peril…for the sake of the greater good." (Stone: 587); p. 41, George Creel: "the world's greatest adventure in advertising." (Thompson: 156); p. 43, Newspaper headline: "taken the Hun out of his name!" (Ferrell: 206); p. 43, Woman's club newsletter reporter: "Jane Addams…becoming a bore. (Capozzola: 149).

CHAPTER 4—HOLD YOUR TONGUE

OPENING QUOTE: p. 45, Thomas Hardwick: "In times of war…contagion of hysteria." (Stone: 189).

RAISED QUOTE: p. 53, Editorial, *Northwestern Christian Advocate*: "The gospel of hate. . . . tactics of Germany herself." ("Is Hatred of the German…": 384).

PHOTO CAPTIONS: p. 47, German-American saying: "Germany my mother; America my bride." (Capozzola: 181); p. 48, *Bisbee Daily Review:* "display of patriotism and high-minded public spirit." ("The Great Wobbly Drive"); p. 48, Sheriff Harry Wheeler: "those strange men…from other parts." (American Mining Congress); p. 54, *New York World:* "The bureaucrats…reign of terror in the U.S." (Stone: 181).

TEXT: p. 46, Participant in the lynching of Robert Prager: "one for the red, one for the white, and one for the blue." (Capozzola: 117); p. 46, Theodore Roosevelt: "not Americans at all. . . . servants of Germany." (Hawley: 29); p. 49, Harry Wheeler: "Perhaps everything I did wasn't legal." (Capozzola: 128); p. 49, Justice Department agent: "Miss Brundage…13 years of age. (Capozzola: 185); p. 50, Bar patron: Germany was "all right." (Capozzola: 158); p. 51, WW: "Every American who takes part…no true son of this great Democracy." (Capozzola: 118); pp. 51-52, U.S. Commissioner of Education: "The United States…language or literature." (Nollendorfs: 176); p. 52, American Defense Society: "is not a fit language…boys and girls." (Capozzola: 181); p. 55, H. L. Mencken: "Between Wilson and his brigades…has pretty well vanished in America." (Stone: 156-57).

CHAPTER 5—BETWEEN WAR AND PEACE

OPENING QUOTE: p. 56, WW: "Any man who resists…his human kind forever." (Brands: 108).

RAISED QUOTE: p. 64, WW: "I have found… without fighting for it." (Thompson: 220).

PHOTO CAPTIONS: p. 57, Jane Addams: I see no reason why…in time of peace." (Capozzola: 148); p. 59, Campaign slogan: "For President—Convict #9653." (Stone: 198); p. 64, the *New York Times:* "The spirit of the crowd seemed at times akin to fanaticism." (Brands: 121).

TEXT: p. 58, WW: "A supreme moment. . . . laid upon the nations." (Brands: 98); p. 62, Protest signs: "Mr. President…Safe for Democracy?" and "Bring Democracy…to Europe." (Ferrell: 217); p. 63, WW: "making good what they offered their life's blood to obtain." (Thompson: 196); p. 63, H.G. Wells: "He ceased to be a common statesman; he became a Messiah." (Thompson: 2); p. 63, Newspaper headline: "The Moses from Across the Atlantic." (Brands: 104); p. 66, Ike Hoover: "sicker than the world ever knew. . . . simply impossible." (Crunden: 272); p. 66, Robert Lansing: "If it ever gets out it will make a fine scandal." (Brands: 130).

AFTERWORD

OPENING QUOTE: p. 68, Henry Steele Commager: "If there is any moral to be drawn. . . . is neither necessary nor wise." (Stone: 239).

TEXT: p. 72, WW: "There will come a time. . . . peoples of the world." (Brands: 121); p. 73, WW: "We are provincials no longer. . . . the principles of a liberated mankind." (Brands: 138-39).

GUIDE TO WARTIME PRESIDENCIES

RAISED QUOTES: p. 74, Abigail Adams: "I wish the laws of our country. . . . kept over foreigners." (Adams: 179); p. 74, James Madison: "Some degree of abuse…over error and oppression." (*The Debates in the Several State Conventions…*: 571); p. 75, Abraham Lincoln: "I may not have made…as well as anyone could." (Herndon: 319); p. 76, WW: "I am in a hurry. . . . effects of that opinion." ("Wilson Calls for American Line-Up": 1,6);

p. 76, Elmer Davis: "A democracy fighting a total war…comfort to the enemy." (Stone: 279-80); p. 77, Harry S. Truman: "Scaremongers and the hate mongers. . . . all Americans are in peril." (Public Papers of the Presidents, Harry S. Truman Library: online resource); p. 78, Richard M. Nixon: "To you, the great silent majority. . . . Only Americans can do that." (Woolley and Peters, address by Richard Nixon: online resource); p. 78, George W. Bush: "Americans are a free people. . . . God's gift to humanity." (Woolley and Peters, address by George W. Bush: online resource).

PHOTO CAPTIONS: p. 77, Ronald Reagan: "tear down this wall." (Boyd).

INDEX

ILLUSTRATIONS CREDITS

Grateful acknowledgment is made for the use of images from the following sources. Illustrations preceded by the initials LC are reproduced courtesy the Library of Congress Prints and Photographs Division; images from the Wisconsin Historical Society are abbreviated as WHi; images marked NYT are from the *New York Times*, © date of publication the *New York Times* All rights reserved. Used by permission and protected by the Copyright Laws of the United States. The printing, copying, redistribution, or retransmission of the Material without express written permission is prohibited.

Front cover, Jason Todd/The Image Bank/Getty Images; opening endpaper, NYT, © 5-8-1915; p. 2, Istockphoto.com; p. 8, LC-USZ62-85704; pp. 10-11, Bettman/CORBIS; p. 13, SEF/Art Resource; pp. 14-15, upper, LC-USZ62-64956; pp. 14-15, middle, LC-DIG-ggbain-17779; p. 15, LC-USZ62-138941; p. 16, upper, LC-DIG-ggbain-01923; p. 16, lower, LC-USZ62-138940; pp. 16-17, LC-DIG-ggbain-17780; p. 18, Jason Todd/The Image Bank/Getty Images; pp. 18-19, Snark Art Resource; p. 19, Ullstein Bild/akg-images 00008809; p. 20, LC-USZ62-118927; p. 21, LC-USZ62-118926; pp. 22-23, LC-USZ62-118464; pp. 22, LC-USZ62-130131; p. 24, Art Resource; pp. 26-27, LC-USZ62-113662; p. 27, LC-USZ62-21328; pp. 28-29, LC-DIG-ggbain-11185; p. 29, LC-USZC4-10930; p. 30, upper, Jason Todd/The Image Bank/Getty Images; p. 30, lower, LC-USZ62-38141; pp. 30-31, LC-USZ62-37781; p. 32, LC-USZ62-96416; p. 33, upper, LC-DIG-ggbain-20705; p. 33, lower, LC-DIG-ggbain-20622; p. 35, LC-USZC4-11966; p. 36, LC-USZ62-36583; p. 37, LC-USZ62-48843; p. 38, Stapleton Collection/CORBIS; pp. 38-39, LC-USZ62-48222; p. 40, left, LC-USZC4-10652; p. 40, right, LC-USZC4-9851; p. 42, upper, author's collection; p. 42, lower, LC-DIG-ggbain-18848; p. 43, Jason Todd/The Image Bank/Getty Images; p. 44, The Museum of Modern Art/Licensed by SCALA/Art Resource; pp. 46-47, WHi-30364; p. 47, LC-USZ62-48226; p. 48, National Archives and Records Administration, ARC 2739188, Josephine Weissenberger; pp. 48-49, LC-USZ62-63631; p. 50, LC-USZ62-7481; p. 51, Getty Images; p. 53, upper, WHi-24404; p. 53, lower, WHi-3455; p. 54, left, LC-DIG-hec-02451; p. 54, right, LC-DIG-hec-02102; p. 57, HIP/Art Resource; p. 59, left, Bettman/CORBIS; p. 59, right, Bettman/CORBIS; p. 59, lower, Underwood & Underwood/CORBIS; pp. 60-61, LC-DIG-ggbain-29368; p. 61, LC-DIG ppmsca-05647; p. 62, LC-USZ62-36185; p. 63, Jason Todd/The Image Bank/Getty Images; p. 64, LC-DIG ppmsca-13425; pp. 64-65, LC call # PR 13 CN 1976:193 or digital ID pan 6a36772; pp. 66-67, Bettman/CORBIS; p. 67, LC-USZ62-85706; pp. 68-69, detail from poster ("Many peoples one nation—Let us unite to Americanize America") LC-USZC4-7389; p. 71, Bettman/CORBIS; p. 72, Jason Todd/The Image Bank/Getty Images; p. 73, Bettman/CORBIS; p. 74, left, LC-DIG-ppmsca-15705; p. 74, right, LC-USZ62-16960; p. 75, upper, LC-USZ62-107577; p. 75, lower, LC-USZ62-2276; p. 76, LC-USZ62-104520; p. 77, Dirk Halstead/Time Life Pictures/Getty Images; p. 78, left, Rolls Press/Popperfoto/Getty Images; p. 78, right, Charles Ommanney Getty Images; closing endpaper, NYT, © 9-12-2001; back cover, adapted from poster ("I want YOU for U.S. Army") LC-USZC4-594.

Founded in 1888, the National Geographic Society is one of the largest nonprofit scientific and educational organizations in the world. It reaches more than 285 million people worldwide each month through its official journal, NATIONAL GEOGRAPHIC, and its four other magazines; the National Geographic Channel; television documentaries; radio programs; films; books; videos and DVDs; maps; and interactive media. National Geographic has funded more than 8,000 scientific research projects and supports an education program combating geographic illiteracy.

For more information, please call 1-800-NGS LINE (647-5463) or write to the following address:

National Geographic Society
1145 17th Street N.W., Washington, D.C.
20036-4688 U.S.A.

Visit us online at
www.nationalgeographic.com/books

For librarians and teachers:
www.ngchildrensbooks.com

More for kids from National Geographic:
kids.nationalgeographic.com

For information about special discounts for bulk purchases, please contact National Geographic Books Special Sales: ngspecsales@ngs.org

For rights or permissions inquiries, please contact National Geographic Books Subsidiary Rights: ngbookrights@ngs.org